LeaderSHOP

Volume One

Workplace, Career, and Life Advice
From Today's Top Thought Leaders

Dr. Rodger Dean Duncan

Maxwell Stone
PUBLISHING

ACCLAIM FOR
LeaderSHOP
Volume One

"Rodger Dean Duncan's previous book *CHANGE-friendly LEADER-SHIP* is a goldmine of actionable wisdom. With *LeaderSHOP,* he continues to pass out the gold nuggets."
- **Jack Canfield**
Co-creator of *Chicken Soup for the Soul*

"This is a remarkable book of remarkable insights by remarkable people. *LeaderSHOP* should be read and re-read by anyone who's serious about personal development."
- **Adam Kirk Smith**
Author of *The Bravest You*

"Any book that can help you save just one employee is worth the cover price many times over. By that measure, *LeaderSHOP* is worth a fortune."
- **Corrie Shanahan**
Author of *Do It Mean It Be It*

"In a world filled with dubious advice on success, *LeaderSHOP* stands out as the real deal. These experts cut to the chase in offering smart ideas on moving from where you are to where you want and need to be."
- **Herbert M. Baum**
Former President of Campbell Soup Company, CEO of Quaker State, and Chairman of The Dial Corporation

"*LeaderSHOP* is a breath of fresh air. Whether you're a new leader, an experienced leader, or someone hoping to grow into a leadership role, this book is packed with tangible takeaways you can put into action immediately."
- **Molly Beck**
Founder of Messy.fm and author of *Reach Out*

"When it comes to personal and organization effectiveness, Rodger Dean Duncan knows the smart questions to ask. In this user-friendly volume, he and his band of thought leaders provide answers that inform, inspire, entertain, and sometimes surprise. *LeaderSHOP* is a book you should read often."
   - **Dr. Brent D. Peterson**
   Co-author of *Fake Work: Why People Are Working Harder Than Ever But Accomplishing Less, and How to Fix the Problem*

"The hallmark of a great mind is to investigate and serve up truth. Rodger's done this in his inimitable style, compiling some of the most important truths in business and life by teaming up with a pantheon of other powerful thought leaders."
   - **Barry Rellaford**
   Executive Coach, author of *A Slice of Trust*

"'Must-read' is a cliché applied to some books that don't deserve it. This one does. If career and life success are priorities for you, *Leader-SHOP* should be at the top of your reading list."
   - **Nancy Lauterbach**
   Former president, International Association of Speakers Bureaus

"Dialogue is the oxygen of change, improvement, and employee engagement. The conversations in *LeaderSHOP* will increase your capacity as a leader and manager that will deliver immediate results. This book is a must for your leadership library!"
   - **John Stoker**
   Founder of DialogueWORKS, author of *Overcoming Fake Talk*

"*LeaderSHOP* is a great resource for anyone in today's world of work. Rodger is an excellent interviewer and his conversations with Blue Chip thought leaders provide fascinating insights and great ideas. Very enjoyable."
   - **David E. Nielson**
   Author of *The 9 Dimensions of Conscious Success*

"*LeaderSHOP* gives valuable guidance for learning moments. Rodger Dean Duncan and his impressive group of thought leaders help accelerate learning our way to success."
- **Julia Tang Peters**
  Author of *Pivot Points: Five Decisions Every Successful Leader Must Make*

"*LeaderSHOP* is a master class with master teachers. Be sure to show up, take careful notes, and practice your learnings. Your life will improve if you do."
- **Pat Obuchowski**
  CEO of inVisionaria, author of *Gutsy Women Win*

"The experts in *LeaderSHOP* show you the principles, practices, and behaviors that will help you soar to success. Read it. Learn from it. Then go lead!"
- **Jacqueline M. Stavros and Cheri B. Torres**
  Co-authors of *Conversations Worth Having*

"*LeaderSHOP* is a stunningly valuable book. Every chapter provides great ideas and tools from the world's top leadership experts that will bring more success to your business, career, and life. I learned a lot from this book. You will too."
- **John Spence**
  Author of *Awesomely Simple* and *Strategies for Success*

"Just when you think there's little new to say about leadership and personal development, *LeaderSHOP* breaks the mold. This book addresses virtually every concern that people have in today's workplace."
- **Peter Rail**
  Founding President, National Association of Employee Concerns Professionals

"*LeaderSHOP* provides crisp insights from outstanding experts, a great guide for leaders at every stage of the journey."
- **Jeffrey E. Thompson, MD**
  Author of *Lead True: Live Your Values, Build Your People, Inspire Your Community*

"*LeaderSHOP* is full of aha moments and jam packed with practical and immediately usable insights."
- **Kelly Palmer**
Former Chief Learning Officer at LinkedIn and Yahoo!, co-author of *The Expertise Economy*

In *LeaderSHOP*, Rodger Dean Duncan explores the most important workplace issues of our time—and he does it in candid conversations with dozens of experts whose ideas will touch both your heart and your mind. Rodger is both an excellent writer and great thinker. Don't miss his latest book!"
- **Bonnie Hagemann**
Author of *Leading With Vision*

"Leadership is forged in the crucible of experience. You can enhance your own experience through learning from others. In *Leader-SHOP* you get the benefit of seasoned experts who reveal the keys to unlocking your potential."
- **John Davis**
Managing Partner, The Cramer Institute

"Above all, great leaders give: Generously, selflessly, and without expectation of return. Why? Because their success results from the success of others. As for *what* great leaders give... the incredible people represented in *LeaderSHOP* have all the answers."
- **Jeff Haden**
Inc. contributing editor and author of *The Motivation Myth: How High Achievers Really Set Themselves Up to Win*

"Rodger Dean Duncan gets it! In his own work and writing, he strikes the perfect chord in coaching people to personal effectiveness. In *LeaderSHOP* he's joined by dozens of other thought leaders who share practical wisdom. Read it. Use it."
- **Norm Smallwood**
Co-author of *Leadership Sustainability* and other books

"*LeaderSHOP* is your one-stop resource of great leadership thinking. Whether you want a quick tip or a deep dive, Rodger Dean Duncan offers a full menu of insight and advice you can use immediately."
   - Doug Sterbenz
   Author of *Must Be Present to Win*

"Personal effectiveness is both an art and a science. Readers of *LeaderSHOP* get the benefit of both artists and scientists—top thought leaders who clearly know what they're talking about."
   - Garry Ridge
   President & CEO of WD-40 Company

"In *LeaderSHOP*, Rodger Dean Duncan continues his focus on who professional people should be, not just what they do. Regardless of where you are in your career, this is a book you should carefully read and digest."
   - Dr. Timothy R. Clark
   Author of *Leading With Character and Competence*

"Insightful. Instructive. Inspiring. That's my three-word endorsement of *LeaderSHOP*."
   - Liane Davey
   Author of *You First: Inspire Your Team to Grow Up, Get Along, and Get Stuff Done*

Experts

Table of Contents

MEANING AND PURPOSE

MENTAL MAPS

WORKPLACE PRACTICES

FEEDBACK AND ACCOUNTABILITY

COMMUNICATION

CAREER MANAGEMENT

PERSONAL BALANCE

Foreword

By Marshall Goldsmith

Marshall Goldsmith is the *Thinkers 50* #1 Executive Coach and the only two-time #1 Leadership Thinker in the World.

He's the bestselling author of *Triggers, Mojo,* and *What Got You Here Won't Get You There.*

It's been said that if you inspire others to *dream* more, *learn* more, *do* more, and *become* more, you're a leader.

This volume by Rodger Dean Duncan does all of that and then some. The "then some" is that it focuses on what you can do for *yourself.*

The subject of "leadership" encompasses a mind-boggling array of principles and practices. And one thing is certain: true leadership has nothing whatsoever to do with the size of your office or the title on your door. It's all about your influence for good in the lives of people around you. Whether you're striving to be more effective with colleagues in the boardroom or with loved ones at your kitchen table, *LeaderSHOP* offers tools you can use.

In addition to his own insightful commentaries on subjects ranging from "Your Brain Has a Mind of Its Own" to how to name and tame the elephant in the room, Rodger shares his conversations with some of the brightest thought leaders of our time.

Are you looking for more meaning and purpose in your work? **Bill George** explains how to discover your "True North" and surround yourself with people who can help bring out your best.

Do you sometimes get down on yourself and doubt your potential? **Elizabeth B. Crook** shows you how to buck your barriers and discover the "Yippee!" that can push you upward and onward.

Is your workplace stifled by office politics? **Rob Fazio** offers sound advice on dealing with dysfunctional colleagues without taking things personally or becoming a victim.

Do you know that some of the behaviors that may help you early in your career can actually jeopardize your advancement later? My colleague **Sally Helgesen** and I talk about habits that curb and habits that lift.

A key task of a good leader is the development, not of followers, but of more good leaders. **Erika Andersen** explains how gardening is the ideal metaphor for this all-important work.

Because trust is critical in all your relationships and business dealings, **Stephen M. R. Covey** offers research-based counsel on how to earn and maintain trust, and how to maximize its positive impact on your career and your business.

Even leaders report to somebody: another leader, stockholders, etc. **Mary Abbajay** reveals how to deal with an incompetent or troubling manager by "managing up" in ways that enhance rather than derail your career.

Do you wish you had more hours in the day? **Brian Tracy** shows how to beat the time crunch by avoiding the "reactive-responsive" mode, the "attraction distraction" and other traps that put your productivity and life balance at risk.

Are you searching for ways to get more traction with your good ideas? **Carmine Gallo** illustrates how your next presentation can benefit from the "less really is more" principle.

Are there times when you need to say "No!" in the workplace, but you're not sure how to do it without getting fired? **Ira Chaleff** discloses helpful tips on how to practice "intelligent disobedience."

In trying to influence your coworkers to do better and be better, do you sometimes get frustrated by your lack of authority? **Mark Sanborn** explains some workable influence tactics and why you don't need a title to be a leader.

Do you want members of your team to be really *engaged*? Jim Kouzes spells out the advantages of dialogue over monologue, and explains how to build a genuine sense of community in your workplace.

If you're like most people, "life balance" is more of an aspiration than a reality. **Laura Vanderkam** shows how to get "off the clock" and feel less busy while getting more done. It's simpler than you might imagine.

These and dozens of other conversations make this book a bona fide treasure for anyone seeking greater success at work and in life. Each chapter is a quick read, chock full of wise advice from smart people. I'm honored to be part of it.

This Volume 1 certainly whets my appetite. Now I'm looking forward to Volumes 2, 3 and beyond.

About the Author

Also by Rodger Dean Duncan

Teaching Your Child the Fi$cal Facts of Life

Leadership for Saints

CHANGE-friendly LEADERSHIP

By Small & Simple Things

Rodger Dean Duncan is author of the award-winning internation-al bestseller *CHANGE-friendly LEADERSHIP: How to Transform Good Intentions Into Great Performance.*

His interest in personal development and leadership issues first sprouted when he was a university undergraduate. The interest blossomed into full-scale passion when he covered business and politics as a young journalist. One of his early editors was Jim Lehrer (later of PBS television fame), who taught him how to connect the dots between what people aspire to and what they actually accomplish.

After reporting for *The Salt Lake Tribune, The Fort Worth Star-Telegram,* and *The Dallas Times Herald,* Rodger was managing editor of two daily newspapers in Texas. He also wrote a syndicated column and freelanced for many national magazines.

When he was 28, Rodger launched a consulting practice focusing on leadership and performance improvement issues. His clients have ranged from cabinet officers in two White House administrations to senior leaders in many of the world's best companies in more than a dozen industries. In addition, he headed communications at Campbell Soup Company and was vice president of a global energy firm.

Rodger earned his PhD in organizational dynamics at Purdue University. His personal blog reaches opt-in subscribers in nearly 200 countries. He also writes a regular column for Forbes.com that reaches millions. Bestselling author Stephen R. Covey called Rodger's work in leadership "brilliantly insightful and inspiring; profound, yet user friendly; visionary, yet highly practical."

Rodger and his wife live in Missouri. They are parents of four grown children, and have 12 grandchildren and two great grandchildren.

For a free self-assessment and other bonus items, go to:
www.MyLeaderSHOP.com

Preface

As a young boy, I was curious about most everything around me. I peppered the adults in my life with a barrage of questions: *Why won't fish bite on dead minnows? How do you sharpen a saw? Why are cucumber seeds planted in mounds? What makes thunder and lightning? Is anyone older than God?*

My early teachers, especially my grandfather, always had a patient answer—liberally seasoned with a heavy dose of common sense and sometimes a sprinkle of humor.

I carried that inquisitive nature through my school days and into my adulthood. It served me well as a young journalist when I interviewed interesting people like Lyndon Johnson, comedian Jack Benny, Baroness Maria von Trapp, cardiac surgery pioneer Michael DeBakey, historian Arnold Toynbee, pollster George Gallup, luxury retailer Stanley Marcus, baseball Hall of Famer Harmon Killebrew, and anthropologist Margaret Mead. I later traded jokes with Norman Rockwell and discussed home carpentry with Robert Redford. Of course I've also talked with thousands of not-so-famous people. They've all had stories to tell and opinions to express. I've learned something every time.

Today, most of my interviews are with so-called "thought leaders." They've earned that appellation because their views are taken to be authoritative and influential. They think big and they say things worth hearing.

The conversations reported in this volume—the first in a series—are with some of the smartest people around. I appreciate their generosity in giving me their time as well as their opinions. I believe you'll agree it makes for good reading.

Without a good question, a good answer has no place to go. So I'll keep asking questions.

Rodger Dean Duncan

Meaning and Purpose

"It's very difficult to have a meaningful life without meaningful work."

Jim Collins

For Best Results, Live Life 'Day One' at a Time

Expert: Drew Dudley, serial entrepreneur, recovered alcoholic, university professor, bestselling author

What you'll learn: As the saying goes, "You must be present to win." That's especially true in the way you live your life.

More than 30 years ago I wrote a personal mission statement. It's a relatively brief and straightforward document (less than half a page), focusing on six roles that I identified for my life. I use it as a daily, forward-looking reminder of my commitments, vision, and purpose.

As my friend Stephen Covey used to say, when you live out of memory you focus on the past. When you live out of your imagination you focus on the future.

Of course, there's also value in living in the present. After decades of observing and studying effective people, I've noticed one characteristic that sets them all apart: they have a single-minded devotion to what they want to *be*. Not just what they want to do, but what they want to *be*.

That's the emphasis in Drew Dudley's book *This is DAY ONE: A Practical Guide to Leadership That Matters.*

This is a leadership book with a different twist. It's not about leadership involving position, titles, organization charts or corner office privileges. It's about the day after day behaviors that enable influence and making a positive difference.

Dudley suggests six key values and accompanying questions that will immediately stimulate personal leadership behaviors:

- **Impact**—What have I done today to recognize someone else's leadership?

- **Courage**—What did I try today that might not work, but I tried it anyway?

- **Empowerment**—What did I do today to move someone else closer to a goal?

- **Growth**—What did I do today to make it more likely someone will learn something?

- **Class**—What did I "elevate instead of escalate" today?

- **Self-Respect**—What did I do today to be good to myself?

Using questions like these, Dudley advises, can help people discover, define, and consistently deliver on their foundational leadership values.

Dudley is the former director of the leadership development program at the University of Toronto and coaches for organizations ranging from JP Morgan Chase to Proctor & Gamble. His TED talk was voted "one of the 15 most inspirational TED talks of all time."

I tracked him down for a conversation to explore his thinking on personal leadership.

Rodger Dean Duncan: *In a nutshell, the Day One approach treats leadership as a daily choice, not as a title or accolade earned over time. What are some first steps to adopting this paradigm as an actual practice?*

Drew Dudley: First, don't be dismissive of its simplicity. Simple doesn't mean easy. It's not unusual for high-performers, when presented with the Day One approach, to assume they've already moved beyond what it teaches … until they actually try it. That's when they realize they haven't moved beyond its principles—they've skipped over them.

That's not unusual for most people. The approach focuses on the foundational building blocks of personal leadership, so it's not glitzy. It's the miles of running in the rain before the marathon, or the hours in the gym before stepping into the ring: unglamorous and essential. However, the more committed you are to reinforcing the foundations of your personal leadership each day the more you raise your capacity for high performance.

Second, you must embrace the idea that who you want to be each day should be prioritized over what you have to do. You must be willing to identify and commit to specific personal leadership behaviors that are non-negotiable each day. These behaviors can't be put aside in the name of your to-do list. It's not an either/or situation. A significant tenet of this approach is identifying how you can engage in those behaviors through your work, so it doesn't involve compromising your commitment to your career.

Finally, recognize what the approach does not promise to do. It's not trying to lay out how to become a senior executive or CEO, build high-performing teams, or acquire wealth, power and prominence—at least not directly. It's designed to embed the behaviors necessary to be the type of person who is consistently great at those things.

Duncan: *Leadership, you say, is making your life less about living up to the expectations of others and more about a disciplined commitment to acting on your core values each day. What's a good approach to clarifying what those personal core values really are?*

Dudley: Your key values are indicated by how you behave, not what you say. As such, it's important to surface these values through reflective activities rather than simply asking yourself what they are. I cover this in detail in the book, but the key piece is an assessment of your decisions and behaviors—good and bad—and what values were reflected through those actions.

Our focus often falls on the consequences and outcomes of our decisions rather than the values that drove them. My goal is to help people shift that focus, and in doing so reveal potential inconsistencies between the values you believe drive you and those that actually do.

Duncan: *You suggest that each core value a person identifies for himself should be accompanied by a question. That clearly serves as a daily call to action. Any other reasons for the questions?*

Dudley: The questions are what set the Day One approach apart. The book doesn't necessarily aim to teach you things you don't know about leadership. It's intended to lay out a practical process to translate your knowledge of what makes a good leader into actual *actions*. The questions are an essential part of that for three key reasons:

1. They demand specificity—the questions outlined in the book are constructed in a very particular way: they cannot be answered yes or no, but demand you are specific in the what, when and how you engaged in certain behaviors.

2. They draw on psychological research that leverages unconscious drivers of human behavior, supporting your conscious efforts to deliver on your personal leadership commitments.

3. They allow for a daily assessment of your personal

leadership—a daily "leadership test" that speaks to your success at aligning your key leadership values with your behavior.

Duncan: *What role does courage play in living a Day One life?*

Dudley: Courage is essential for growth, innovation, and resilience. However, we may not realize how our daily commitment to courage is eroded as we move through an education system that villainizes mistakes and stresses compliance over courage. The Day One process aims to re-embed courage as a daily practice—ensuring you consistently challenge the status quo in ways that benefit you and your organization.

Leaders are often afraid. But they don't let fear lead to inaction. The Day One approach frames courage as a commitment to taking action when there is the possibility of loss. It recognizes that while the potential loss may be something tangible—money, a job, or an opportunity—it's more often than not a perceived loss—a loss of face, of respect or prestige in the eyes of others. The Day One approach doesn't ask you to simply "get over" that fear, but rather offers specific strategies to challenge that fear daily.

Duncan: *Many people seem to view life as a zero-sum game with winners and losers. How does the Day One approach help replace that scarcity mentality with something better?*

Dudley: The scarcity mindset focuses on money, titles, and influence as goals. The Day One approach positions them not as goals but as the *natural by-products* of consistent value-based behavior. Most importantly, it provides a process for ensuring that consistency.

The Day One approach fully embraces an important reality: you're not always in charge of what you have to do every day, but you're always in charge of *who you are*. It doesn't deny that winning and losing is a fundamental part of our lives and careers or ask you to simply reframe losses as "wins because you learned something." It provides clear daily goals over which you *do* have complete control—goals that can provide momentum even on the days where everything outside of your control personally and professionally blows up in your face.

Duncan: *What happens when we challenge traditional definitions and redefine what leadership really is?*

Dudley: We ruffle some feathers. People who have worked 90 hours per week and sacrificed their relationships for a corner office or dropped 150 grand on a degree sometimes see a broader definition of leadership as inferring "you're not so special after all," and push back. I'm not trying to devalue traditional definitions of leadership or tell anyone who's worked hard to get ahead or set themselves apart that they are any less impressive or deserving of what they've achieved. What I am arguing is that there is a form of leadership to which everyone can and should aspire, and that many individuals who are considered "successful" have dismissed as unimportant. By defining leadership so narrowly for so long, we've ensured that the majority of people in our organizations minimize their potential impact on the organization, clients, and colleagues. At the same time, many people who occupy C-Suites can't define their core leadership values or identify a single act they undertook today to live up to those values.

When we reframe leadership as being evaluated on a daily basis—determined solely by how any one person is behaving *today*, not what they've accomplished over time—we reinforce the idea that everyone starts at the same place each day: with an obligation (and the ability) to positively impact the people, organizations, and communities around them.

Personal application:

- Have you written a personal mission statement? It can help clarify your values.

- What behaviors seem to produce the results you want? How can you practice those behaviors more consistently?

- At the end of each day, how do you honestly evaluate how you've lived the past 24 hours?

2

The Why of Work: Purpose and Meaning on the Job

Experts: David Ulrich and Wendy Ulrich, consultant and psychologist, world-class coaches, bestselling authors

What you'll learn: Everyone in the workplace has responsibility for giving purpose and meaning to the enterprise. Leaders have a special role in modeling.

Why?

It's a question all of us should ask ourselves. Why do we do what we do? In particular, why do we do the work that, for many of us, occupies most of our waking hours for our entire adult lives?

Ralph Waldo Emerson left us a quote worthy of one of those inspirational wall posters: "The purpose of life is not to be happy. It is to be useful, to be honorable, to be compassionate, to have it make some difference that you have lived and lived well."

That thought may feel warm and fuzzy, but the question remains: Why do we do the work we do?

Dave and Wendy Ulrich address that and many related issues in *The Why of Work: How Great Leaders Build Abundant Organizations That Win.*

Dave Ulrich, professor of business at the University of Michigan, has authored or coauthored more than 30 books that have shaped the human resources profession and the field of leadership development. Wendy Ulrich is a psychologist, educator and writer with a passion for helping people create healthy relationships and meaning-rich lives.

I visited with this dynamic duo to explore their thinking on issues affecting engagement, productivity, and—yes—purpose and meaning in the workplace.

Rodger Dean Duncan: *In the context of meaning in the workplace, how do you define abundance?*

David Ulrich: Abundance is to have a fullness (e.g., an abundant harvest) or to live life to its fullest (e.g., an abundant life).

An abundant organization enables its employees to be completely fulfilled by finding meaning and purpose from their work experience. This meaning enables employees to have personal hope for the future and create value for customers and investors. When we ask people how they feel about their work, we can quickly get a sense of how work helps them fulfill the things that matter most in their lives.

Duncan: *You point out that meaning and abundance are more about what we do with what we have than about what we have to begin with or what we accumulate. How can a leader persuade people to adopt that viewpoint and to "operationalize" it in the workplace?*

Wendy Ulrich: Clearly this won't fly if a leader is trying to talk people into ignoring bad working conditions when something could be done to change them. But I learned long ago with therapy clients that their misery often had less to do with their circumstances and more to do with what they told themselves those circumstances meant about them. ("This means I'll never be happy …. my future is hopeless ... people don't like me ... I'll never succeed.") Fortunately, even when we cannot change our circumstances, we do control what we tell ourselves those circumstances mean about us. Checking out what is real, changing the story, seeing a different perspective, or getting creative can turn a problem into an opportunity.

Duncan: *How can an organization institutionalize, not merely individualize, abundance and meaning in the workplace?*

David Ulrich: The concept of abundant organizations draws on many diverse literatures related to the employee experience at work: positive psychology, high performing teams, culture, commitment, learning, civility, growth mindset. By distilling these literatures, we identified seven principles of the abundant organization (identity, purpose, relationships/teamwork, positive work environment, personalizing work, resilience/growth, and delight/civility). These principles are institutionalized into organizations by designing and delivering HR practices around people, performance, information, and work that enable organizations to create a personality that outlasts any single individual.

Duncan: *You say leaders are meaning makers. In terms of observable behaviors, what does that look like?*

Wendy Ulrich: People find meaning when they see a clear connection between what they highly value and what they spend time doing. That connection is not always obvious, however. Leaders are in a great position to articulate the values a company is trying to enact and to shape the story of how today's work connects with those values. This means sharing stories of how the company is making a difference for good in the lives of real people, including customers, employees, and communities.

Leaders operationalize that by formally and informally sharing those stories, speaking passionately about what the company stands for and sharing personal lessons learned in that process. Leaders can involve employees in both articulating those values and creating plans to act on them. One way to make those stories come alive is to bring in people who have been helped by the company's products or services and letting them share their stories. We are usually pretty good at sharing financial data. Often more motivating to employees are stories about human impact.

Duncan: *As the story goes, people feel differently about the meaning of their work if they see themselves as bricklayers rather than as building a cathedral to God. What can leaders (and individuals) do to make work more about cathedral-building?*

David Ulrich: There is an old fable of the three bricklayers all working on the same wall. Someone asked the bricklayers, "What you are doing?" The first said "I am laying bricks"; the second bricklayer replied, "I am building a wall"; and the third answered, "I am building a great cathedral for God." The third had a vision of how the daily tasks of laying bricks fit into a broader, more meaningful purpose. Likewise, employees who envision the outcomes of their daily routines find more meaning from doing them. I am not just presenting a lecture as I teach, but preparing the next generation of business leaders.

Duncan: *What advice do you give workers who don't have a charismatic leader who pushes an abundance agenda? What can they do to flourish?*

David Ulrich: Martin Seligman's exceptional book *Flourish* suggests that employees can acquire a more positive outlook on their work by having Positive emotion, Engagement, Relationships, Meaning, and Accomplishments (what he calls PERMA). When employees take personal accountability for creating these attributes (which relate to our seven dimensions of abundance) they do not depend on the leader, but themselves for their work experience. Leaders matter to employee experience, but employee responsibility for the experience matters more. Children mature when they no longer depend on parents to provide all their needs. Likewise, mature employees become agents for their own development.

Duncan: *In the spirit of the Olympic athlete in Chariots of Fire, how can a person find abundant forms of accomplishment? (Insight, Achievement, Connection, Empowerment)*

David Ulrich: Defining what matters most or what success looks like is an easy question that is not simple to answer. Success varies by person and over time for any individual person. Olympic athlete Eric Liddell of *Chariots of Fire* fame started with success in his achievements (I can run fast enough to win the medal), but then morphed to insight (I run to find the pleasure God granted me), and ultimately to empower others (I can help others run to find their purpose). Likewise, an employee can continually ask "what do I want?" and "how do I define success?" These reflection questions helps take personal accountability for their work and personal lives.

Duncan: *Gallup research shows that employees who have a best friend at work are seven times more likely to be highly engaged at work than those who don't. What can be done to create a workplace that fosters those kinds of relationships?*

Wendy Ulrich: Plenty!

Leaders can model healthy relationships at work.

They can encourage people to get to know each other by making time, space, and resources available for them to do so.

They can try to catch people in the act of being nice, thanking and encouraging them.

They can set up ways to teach and coach people in the skills of good relating, such as good listening, being curious about others, apologizing effectively, controlling anger, and letting go of slights—some of the specific skills people can learn and practice that will help them enjoy others and be easier to like.

People with the skills to create and maintain friendship will likely experience less stress at home, increased effectiveness with customers, and improved communications throughout the organization.

Duncan: *What role does personal humility play in a leader's ability to inspire others and create meaning in the workplace?*

Wendy Ulrich: Recent work by Dacher Keltner at UC Berkeley on the dynamics of power is fascinating in this regard. He found that people are most likely to rise to power when they have qualities like kindness, good listening, concern for the greater good, enthusiasm, focus, high empathy, and humility. He also found that once people are in power positions, those qualities too often take a back seat to self-entitlement, indifference to the plight of others, negative interruptions in conversation, and ignoring even basic politeness.

When a leader manages to hold on to his or her humanity and humility even when in the power seat, modeling the highest ideals we have for ourselves as human beings, others want to join that team. Humility is at the heart of a growth mindset that encourages and models learning instead of defensiveness in the face of setbacks, paving the way for creativity and resilience.

Duncan: *Conflict, even if rare, is inevitable in most any work setting. What have you seen as best practices in addressing conflict so the "why" of work is appropriately reinforced?*

Wendy Ulrich: Conflict is not only inevitable, it is valuable, bringing problems to light and different viewpoints to bear on problems. But conflict can also be destructive if not handled with fairness, respect, and good will.

When there's a problem it's almost always best to bring it up in a straightforward way directly with the person involved. If we are contemptuous, critical, or cruel we can expect to get defensiveness and anger in return. If we are calm, curious, and compassionate as we try to both explain our point of view and listen to others, conflict can help us get to better outcomes for all. It's amazing how healing it can be to simply feel genuinely heard and cared about and to receive a respectful apology. Most people will listen if they don't feel threatened or attacked.

Duncan: *How can people find intrinsic value in their work if it's not readily apparent to them?*

Wendy Ulrich: Take a careful look at your deepest values for how to treat other people (especially in the face of disagreement), what matters most in life, what problems you like to solve or want to solve, or what personal strengths are most meaningful to you to contribute to others. Then actively look for ways to live those values, even in small ways, in the everyday work you do.

Living with meaning and purpose is not easy. It may not make us happy in the moment. It requires self-reflection, effort, getting our hands dirty, and struggling with problems that can make us feel frustrated and inadequate. But when we connect with people, remember humor and playfulness, practice creativity and resilience, and go into work situations with a plan, we'll find ample opportunities to practice the values and skills that get us closer to what we want our lives to stand for. That's the intrinsic value of our work.

Duncan: *How should leaders serve as models for meaning in the workplace?*

David Ulrich: When we ask workshop participants to identify leaders who shaped their lives, everyone can quickly name someone. These leaders generally model the principles of abundance in their personal lives and work to instill them in others. Leaders who are meaning-makers are acutely aware of how their good intentions need to show up in good behaviors; how their daily interactions need to reflect their personal values; and how their job as a leader is not just to be personally authentic, but to help others develop their authenticity.

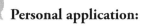

Personal application:

- What can you do to demonstrate kindness and empathy in your workplace?

- With regard to your own work, how do you define purpose and meaning?

- How can you help your co-workers feel a greater sense of meaning in their work (service to customers and end-users, etc.)?

3

Discover Your True North

Expert: Bill George, Harvard professor, bestselling author, former executive at Honeywell and Litton Industries, chairman at Medtronic

What you'll learn: "Authentic" leaders have self-awareness, which requires honest feedback and clarity about personal values.

For any leader at any level in any organization, clarity of purpose is a critical ingredient of success. In other words, you must know where you're headed and why you're headed there.

A compass provides the ideal metaphor. Just as a compass points toward a magnetic field, your personal "true north" directs your path and pulls you forward.

That's the thesis of *Discover Your True North* by Bill George.

George is so much more than a mere theorist. He's been in the trenches and understands the nuances of leadership practices. He started his career in the U.S. Department of Defense, then served in senior executive positions at Honeywell and Litton Industries. George was later president and chairman at Medtronic, one of the world's largest medical equipment and development companies. He's served on boards at ExxonMobile, Novartis, Target, and the Mayo Clinic. Today he teaches leadership at the Harvard Business School.

Rodger Dean Duncan: *You write about "authentic" leadership. What is it in our society that seems to cause people to equate "celebrity" with authenticity?*

Bill George: The media. The media play up celebrity in so many ways. Many of the media people themselves are turned into celebrities. Politicians attempt to be celebrities. The problem is that they're more concerned about the external impressions they make than who they are inside. This is a very serious problem for leaders. In the 1990s the media got caught up with business celebrities and tried to turn a lot of business leaders into celebrities and—judging by all the financial crises we had—many of them did not do well. It's more important to look at the person within and assess their leadership qualities based on who they are as individuals as they move into leadership roles.

Duncan: *I suspect that phenomenon affects people's investment decisions, and that can be dangerous.*

George: Yes, particularly regarding mergers and acquisitions. Unfortunately, many people get drawn into doing acquisitions because of external pressures. They want to make a big hit or a big splash or a big impression.

Duncan: *Doing what's possibly a good thing but for the wrong reasons.*

George: Exactly. And you do get a lot of media attention when you do a big acquisition. Unfortunately, when some leaders can't grow their businesses organically they start to look for ways to make a big splash with acquisitions.

Duncan: *And we've all seen the statistics that show most acquisitions fail to measure up to the performance promised in the initial hype.*

George: Yes. They spent more time worrying about the price and projecting cost savings than they did in considering how the two cultures integrate and who will hold the leadership roles in the new organization.

Duncan: *What are some of the more common things that influence people to lose their way—to lose sight of their True North?*

George: It's when they get caught up with extrinsic motivations. The three great seducers are money, fame, and power.

We saw this in the case of Rajat Gupta. He was an exceptional leader but made some big mistakes and went to jail for two years for insider trading. He got caught up in trying to go from being worth $120 million to a billion. He's a good person. But this happens. And people get caught up in their status. Power-based leadership is almost like a drug and people can get addicted to it. Power is not the role of a leader. The leader's true role is to empower others.

Duncan: *You say the dimensions of an authentic leader include Purpose, Values, Relationships, Self-Discipline, and Heart. Relationships certainly evolve over time, and a person's self-discipline is likely to improve with maturity. What about Purpose, Values, and Heart? How do those dimensions evolve?*

George: I think your purpose evolves from life experience. I think it's very hard as a young person to go out and test yourself against the challenges of the real world and to know what your purpose is. I used to think that was first, but then I realized people really need to do a lot of inner work and understand their True North before they can ascertain their purpose. They must understand their life stories and the crucibles they've had. Clarity of purpose often emanates from those experiences.

Duncan: *It seems to me that some pretty solid values must be in place before an individual can even try to clarify his True North.*

George: That's for sure. Your True North is based in the bedrock of your values. There's no question about that. You must be grounded in the values that come out of your life story, your upbringing, what you believe, and how you relate to other people. Your values must be established early.

Duncan: *In the world of business and public life, who are some of today's leaders you regard as demonstrating authenticity? Specifically, what do you see in them that's worth emulating?*

George: I would cite someone like Paul Polman, CEO of Unilever. He's been an exceptionally strong advocate for long-term value created through a multi-stakeholder model. He also advocates the role of sustainability in our products, in our environment, in our lives and in everything we do. He really stands out as a true authentic leader.

Another was Indra Nooyi at PepsiCo. When she took over as CEO in 2006 she immediately established the company's goal as being performance with purpose. She worked to shift the company's portfolio to more healthful foods and beverages.

Duncan: *You write about the transformation from "I" to "We" as being the most important process leaders go through in becoming authentic. What does that transformation look like in observable behaviors?*

George: Almost everything we do as young people is based on individual performance—whether it's grades in school, how we do on tests, etc. Then we go to work and we get judged on individual performance. It's important that we learn to look beyond that.

Leadership is really about how we empower others, how we inspire them to perform at the top level. So we must make that journey from "I" to "We." We must learn that people are not there to serve us. We are there to serve them. This shifts us from top-down leadership to collaborative leadership.

In the "I" model we try to get more power and position. In the "We" model we work to serve others. The "We" model is clearly more effective. With the "We" model, your leadership goes from directing other people to coaching and mentoring other people.

Duncan: *What role does self-awareness play in all this?*

George: Many leaders don't have much self-awareness, and self-awareness is the core of authenticity—of knowing who you are and of knowing your True North. Clarity on your True North requires humility and learning from the crucibles you faced earlier in life. Self-awareness is the key to everything. It definitely can be developed, and leaders need to work on it through honest introspection and receiving honest feedback.

Duncan: *As my grandfather said, "Never turn down a breath mint. Feedback is a gift."*

George: That's certainly true, but some people don't want feedback. And if you don't want it you won't get it. You can remain clueless and just do your own thing.

Duncan: *What are some good ways for a person to identify and confront his or her blind spots?*

George: Honest feedback, especially 360 feedback. Feedback from your boss can certainly be helpful, but feedback from your subordinates and peers can be especially valuable. They see you every day. They see the good, the bad, and the ugly. It's important that you really listen to people trying to give you honest feedback. I'm a big believer in processes that provide written feedback on things that people may not wish to tell you in person.

Duncan: *What kind of support team is most helpful to leaders who genuinely want to be authentic in their behavior?*

George: Having a support team is supremely important. Having at least one person in your life with whom you can be totally open and honest and who will reciprocate is enormously helpful. For me, that's my wife. It's important to have someone who will pull you back down to earth if you're getting too high on yourself and who can provide encouragement if you get too down on yourself.

In addition to that, having good mentors is very helpful—people who will give you honest feedback we talked about earlier.

And third, it's important to have a small group of people with whom you honestly share back and forth. I have a men's group that has met every Wednesday morning for the past 42 years. There are eight guys in there. We also have a couple's group that meets monthly on Sunday night. That kind of interaction is very essential to me.

Personal application:

- Write a personal mission statement that clarifies your core values and indicates specific ways you will live according to those values.

- List three specific things you can do during the coming week to underscore the "we" in your work team and in an important personal relationship.

- Identify—and make an appointment with—a trusted confidant who will give you unvarnished feedback on your blind spots. Repeat regularly.

4

Buck Your Barriers:
Discover Your Yippee!

What you'll learn: Work without passion is drudgery. Find what gets you jazzed and juiced and life will take a very positive turn

Expert: Elizabeth B. Crook, advisor on career and life transitions, author of *Live Large.*

Not everything French novelist Marcel Proust wrote was fiction. One of his observations could be the call to action for any 21st century resident seeking personal reinvention. He said "the real voyage of discovery consists not in seeking new landscapes, but in having new eyes."

Elizabeth B. Crook has made a career of helping people find their new eyes. As head of her own company called Orchard Advisors, Crook helps CEOs and entrepreneurs think and act strategically to grow their companies and enjoy greater personal satisfaction (also known as fun!).

She's shown countless people—Gen Yers to Boomers—how to invent and reinvent themselves. Crook holds degrees from Vanderbilt University and Tennessee State University. A mother and grandmother, she lives on Music Row in Nashville. She's author of *Live Large: The Achiever's Guide to What's Next.*

Rodger Dean Duncan: *How did you begin your journey of helping people discover what they really want to do and be?*

Elizabeth B. Crook: Really by accident. I was working, as I still do, as a business strategist with entrepreneurs and business owners. People frequently called saying, someone told me you are great at helping folks figure things out. Can you help me? I began with an interview so I could understand who they were and what they wanted. Then, depending on their goals, we moved on from there. After working like that with a number of people, I realized three things:

- I was skilled and effective in helping people.
- I loved the feeling of giving people fresh perceptions and possibilities.
- I had actually developed tools and processes that allowed

people to get amazing results!

Duncan: *A lot of people feel trapped in their work. They're either bored silly or they're just putting in time. What advice can you give them?*

Crook: The first advice is get curious.

- Look at the activities you do at work—write each one on a Post-It ® note.
- Sort them. Which ones energize and which ones leave you feeling drained?
- Is there a theme or pattern? Take note.
- Identify which activities you could delegate or streamline.
- Identify how what energizes *you* adds value to your company—and be specific—increases customer retention, reduces accidents, reduces turnaround time, reduces waste, increases productivity etc.
- Schedule a meeting with your boss to talk about how you can add more value. Hint: you will be adding more value if you are doing something you care about.

Duncan: *What are the two or three most common barriers that hold people back from discovering their own Yippee?*

Crook: The single most common barrier people have are their own beliefs—which may or may not be true! Just because people believed the earth was flat didn't make it so!

Your beliefs may have been true at one point in your life but no longer. You may not have been good a math, or there was a sneaky kid in your neighborhood, or you did experience discrimination. This doesn't mean that's still true now.

Yet if I believe it's risky to trust others, then I avoid connecting which will limit my opportunities for new assignments or promotions. This only re-enforces my belief.

If I believe my gender, race, or education level is a barrier that can't be overcome, then I may not even try. Without trying, the barrier that existed in the past or in my mind becomes real.

Duncan: *What advice can you give leaders for creating a Yippee-friendly work environment?*

Crook: Marcus Buckingham, the author of *First Break All the Rules* and a host of other books, says focus on your strengths—those things that make you feel stronger or energized. As a leader, know what gets your people jazzed and juiced, then find a way for them to do more of that. They will bring more passion, extra effort, and value to your company.

Duncan: *As you coach people to perform at the next level, how do you help them discover and cultivate gifts they didn't even know they had?*

Crook: *No pain, no gain!* How many times have we heard that in our lives? It's true about some things like losing weight and saving money—two of the most popular New Year's resolutions. But it's not true for everything. Yet the prevalence of this thinking can make us blind to our own gifts and talents.

We come to believe that unless something is hard, it's not valuable. The truth is when we are using our talents and gifts it feels easy. We tell ourselves that what's easy for us couldn't possibly be valuable. But it is!

At a family gathering I met a cousin, a neuro linguistic researcher, who has spent significant time overseas including China and Saudi Arabia. As she told several of us about the patterns of cancer and other conditions spanning multiple generations, I asked how she was able to figure all this out? She shrugged and replied, "It really wasn't very hard".

Of course it wasn't hard for *her*, because she has a gift of seeing patterns and she can apply that in many fields from language to health!

In order to find your talents and gifts, make a list of the things you know how to do—for example persuade people, organize a project, research a topic, write a report or a story, coordinate an event, see the big picture, take care of the details. Then ask yourself, which of these are energizing for you. In other words, you enjoy doing them.

Our gifts are found at the intersection of what energizes us and what we know how to do. Hint: it's probably something you've been doing in one way or another all your life!

Duncan: *Your father, a pediatrician, reinvented himself as a successful author when he was in his seventies. What did that teach you about self-discovery?*

Crook: In my mid-forties, working in a fast-growth software company, I realized I wanted to make a change. But to what? How could I change direction at that point? Wasn't that something only younger people could do? Then I remembered my father.

He was an energetic and beloved pediatrician in my hometown, driven by a desire to help people, especially children, be healthy. That purpose informed everything he did, from opening an innovative clinic, to writing a national health column, to speaking at conferences all over the country and abroad.

As he got older, he wanted to write about health topics that were not getting addressed. Over the course of years he wrote and published more than a dozen books that changed people's lives. Thirty years later people still tell me my father's books saved their lives and his books still sell!

His purpose was the same; he was merely expressing it in a different form. Plus, he was in his seventies and still going strong doing what he loved.

My 40-something self realized I had plenty of time. And so do you!

Regardless of your age and life stage, your deep purpose and gifts will point you in the direction of all sorts of possibilities for re-discovery.

Duncan: *You talk about the "Triple J" of limiting beliefs and negative self-talk. What is that, and what effect does it have on personal growth? What's the prescription for overcoming it?*

Crook: That would be too risky. You're not experienced enough to take that on. What makes you think they would hire you? Don't even try.

We all have a voice in our head that discourages us, puts us down, scares us or makes us believe we can't be or do all that we can. I call that voice the Triple J—Jury, Judge and Jailer. It passes judgment, sentences us to be less than we are, then locks us up.

The voice expresses the limiting beliefs we have about ourselves and the world. The voice may be the voice of a parent, teacher, coach or someone who was perhaps just trying to protect us from disappointment or even danger when we were young. Or it could be the voice of someone who was threatened by our success. What the voice ignores is that we are competent, responsible adults able to make our own assessments and decisions. But the voice makes us doubt that truth.

So how do we stop the Triple J from "locking us up" and preventing us from achieving our goals? First take a breath and become aware of what the voice is saying—even write it down. It helps to know your enemy. Then start asking yourself questions like these—

1. What am I trying to accomplish? or What do I want to happen?
2. What am I afraid of? Getting clear about this may help you see what's really holding you back. Sometimes it's a

fear of failure, being embarrassed, or having to face you're not perfect.

3. What resources/support both internal and external do I have?
4. Am I willing to face my fears?
5. What would my wisest inner self say? Listen to *that* voice
6. Then go forth and do!

Duncan: *As people progress in their careers they sometimes lose enthusiasm for their work. How can they rekindle interest in their previous "Why" or discover a new "Why" that brings fresh exhilaration to their lives?*

Crook: As our lives and careers evolve we may find ourselves losing the interest and drive in our work that once fueled us. As the saying goes, our get up and go got up and went.

What to do? Discovering or rediscovering our "Why" or purpose is an important first step and it's easier than we think.

Try this. On one side of a sheet write all those jobs or assignments you enjoyed or found fulfilling in some way. Remember this can include volunteer or unpaid work. Opposite each one write why it was satisfying.

When you've finished, look at the Whys running down the page. What are the words or ideas you see repeated?

There may be several words that repeat. A clear statement may emerge or words that hold meaning for you. There is no one right way.

Once you know your purpose, you can use it to guide you to where you can fulfill that purpose and use your gifts and talents while you do so. Now *that* is exhilarating.

Personal application:

- What are the things you're most curious about? Is there a theme or pattern in that list from which you can draw conclusions about possible changes in your life?

- What's at the intersection of what energizes you and what you already know how to do?

- Is there a "Triple J" operating in your life? If so, what can you do about it? What will you do about it?

Mental Maps

"Believe you
can and you're
halfway there."

5

Mindset: It's Really a Lot More Than a Head Game

Commentary: Rodger Dean Duncan

What you'll learn: The image you have of yourself has a profound effect on what you're able to accomplish.

Legions of writers—from Dale Carnegie to Napoleon Hill to Norman Vincent Peale to Anthony Robbins—have touted the value of positive mental attitude. Scores of rah-rah speakers evangelize on the doctrine of believing in ourselves.

All of that is important. But sound thinking requires more than a rosy outlook and a dose of self-esteem. Sound thinking requires a mindset—or orientation—that's both receptive to fresh (even contrary) ideas and accepting of the notion that most of us can be more creative than we've ever dreamed.

When Carol Dweck was a sixth-grader at P.S. 153 in Brooklyn, New York, she experienced something that motivated her to explore why some people view intelligence as a fixed trait while others embrace it as a quality that can be developed and expanded. Young Carol's teacher seated the students around the classroom according to their IQ scores. The boys and girls who didn't have the highest IQs were not trusted to carry the flag during school assemblies. They weren't even allowed to clap erasers or wash the chalkboard or take a note to the principal.

"Our teacher let it be known that IQ for her was the ultimate measure of your intelligence and your character," Carol says. "So the students who had the best seats were always scared of taking another test and not being at the top anymore. It was an uncomfortable thing because you were only as good as your last test score. I think it had just as negative an effect on the kids at the top [as those at the bottom] who were defining themselves in those terms."

Today Carol Dweck is a professor of psychology at Stanford University, having previously taught at Yale, Columbia, and Harvard. Her special interest is in people's self-theories about intelligence and the profound influence such theories have on the motivation to learn. She says people who hold a "fixed" theory are mainly concerned with how smart they are (or are perceived to be). They prefer tasks they can already do well and they tend to avoid tasks on which they may make mistakes and jeopardize their "smart" image.

By contrast, Dr. Dweck says, people who believe in an "expandable" or "growth" theory of intelligence thrive on challenging themselves to increase their abilities, even if they fail at first.

This and related research on intelligence and motivation highlights the role of personal *capacity* in becoming what I refer to as THINK-friendly.

Why was a guy at 3M able to imagine a new use for the sticky-but-not-too-sticky adhesive? Because he was more concerned about solving a problem than about adhering to an arbitrary "that's-not-my-area-of-expertise" paradigm. He *believed* the adage that necessity is the mother of invention, he *believed* he could cook up some workable ideas, and that expansive self-image enabled him to invent Post-It Notes.

How did Steve Jobs and a posse of other smart people transform a computer company into an empire that turned the telephone and music businesses upside down? They refused to be hamstrung by a "fixed" mindset. They knew that most opportunities don't just fall into our laps, we must create them. So they did.

While some people talk about "thinking outside the box," others ask "*What* box?"

Half a century ago Maxwell Maltz aroused the minds of millions with his book *Psycho-Cybernetics*. His primary premise was that many people are trapped in self-images that limit them, while others have self-images that open the door to a cornucopia of possibilities.

Dr. Maltz said that in the human brain there's a sort of motion picture projector, and the "self movie" is played over and over and over again.

If a child is told (especially by a parent, teacher, or other trusted authority figure) that she's clumsy and awkward, there's a good chance she'll regard herself as clumsy and awkward the rest of her life. In fact, she'll likely go out of her way to prove it. If we learn to believe that we're not good at math, that we can't speak with confidence in public, or that we're not comfortable making new friends, all of that will likely be true.

In short, the view we adopt for ourselves profoundly affects the way we lead our lives.

But the good news is that we can deliberately choose to project a different "self movie" on the motion picture screen in our brains. Just like the heroine in the classic children's book *The Little Engine That Could*, we can tell ourselves "I think I can, I think I can, I think I can." And then there's a good chance that, indeed, we *can*.

This does not mean, of course, that a middle-aged couch potato can employ mental gymnastics to transform himself into a professional basketball star. Nor does it mean that a card-carrying pessimist can change the world by merely thinking positive thoughts, or that a tone-deaf piano novice can "will" himself to be the next Beethoven. What it *does* mean is that our intelligence—our mental *capacity*—is not carved in stone.

By rejecting the "fixed" mindset and adopting the "growth" mindset we can cultivate and expand our abilities to develop skills and solve problems that heretofore would have stumped us.

In 1954 Roger Bannister adopted the "growth" mindset to be the first person ever to run a four-minute mile, rebuffing the conventional wisdom that such a feat was anatomically impossible. With the myth shattered, 16 other runners also cracked the four-minute mile over the next three years.

When he was nine, the teachers of our son Baylor told my wife and me that Baylor was a nice little boy but not really capable of excelling in school. (His grades at the time seemed to reinforce that view.)

We thought otherwise. We believed Baylor was simply bored and under-challenged. So we asked the teachers to give him extra assignments. In addition to keeping our boy busier, the extra assignments apparently sent him the message "You're really smart, so here's some additional work to stretch your mind." Baylor began to thrive. His confidence—and his grades—soared. Throughout high school and two university degrees he earned nearly all "A" grades. He now speaks several languages, is a world traveler, and is a diplomat for the U.S. State Department. The turning point was when he jettisoned the "fixed" mindset and adopted the "growth" mindset.

This deliberate and proactive expansion of one's own mental *capacity* is a critical step toward being THINK-friendly. Mindset really is more than a head game. It affects the heart as well.

Personal application:

- List three opinions you have about your own personal abilities that could be hampering your performance.

- Beside each opinion, list a more positive "self movie" you can project in your mind. You might write something like "I'm smart and I know my stuff, so I can learn to speak about it comfortably in public."

- Determine to behave and live according to these new "self movies."

6

Transform Your Mindset, Transform Your Results

Expert: Hugh Blane, advisor to executives and entrepreneurs, author

What you'll learn: Clarifying your purpose can help you avoid a JDTM (Just Doing the Minimum) approach to work.

A balancing act faced by many leaders involves transactional and transformational leadership. It's a balancing act worthy of effort.

Many leaders have an abundance of good *transactional* skills. What they often need is more *transformational* skills—the ability to create a psychological case for action as well as a technical and business case for action.

So what's the difference?

A *transactional* leader focuses on routine and regimented activities. He invests most of his energy in making sure meetings run on time, that administrative details are properly handled, and that completed tasks are noted on checklists. A *transformational* leader focuses primarily on initiating and "managing" change. He influences people to improve, to stretch, and to redefine what's possible.

Transactional things involve making sure the train runs on time. Transformational things involve ensuring that the train is on the right track, that it's headed in the right direction, and that everyone who wants to make the trip has a ticket.

All that may sound like academic gobbledygook. But in the real world of real work, it matters.

Business strategist Hugh Blane lends helpful perspective to the topic. His book is *7 Principles of Transformational Leadership: Create a Mindset of Passion, Innovation, and Growth.*

Rodger Dean Duncan: *You write about a mindset you call JDTM—Just Doing the Minimum. What contributes to that perspective among individual workers and in a workplace culture?*

Hugh Blane: The number one contributor is lack of purpose. For employees or leaders to engage in doing their very best work they must have fallen in love with a hope, dream or aspiration that, when done well, creates value for customers. When they do, they are more enthusiastic, exert more energy, and are vastly more persistent in overcoming obstacles and breaking down barriers to underperformance. These are the employees who are running *to* work in the morning because of the contribution they want to make.

There are also employees who are running *from* work at the end of the day. They run from work because they are not passionate about their work, so the demands of their job become a burden. These employees don't have a purpose that's compelling so they do only enough work to keep their jobs and not get fired. But, there is no fire in the belly and they are simply going through the motions of work.

Duncan: *What are a leader's most productive tools in combating a JDTM mindset?*

Blane: Leaders must have a leadership purpose that is noble, uplifting and that enables employee flourishing. This eradicates the JDTM mindset and converts an employee's mindset away from accepting the minimum to encouraging the maximum.

Duncan: *Many people simply feel overwhelmed in the workplace. What contributes to that and what can leaders do to help relieve the pressure without compromising productivity?*

Blane: There are three contributors to feeling overwhelmed. A negative mindset, an indifferent heartset, and a poor skillset. A negative mindset says "this isn't fair," an indifferent heartset says "I'm really not committed to my company and my work," and a poor skillset says "I don't know how to do this." When all three are present the likelihood of feeling overwhelmed is guaranteed.

Leaders can relieve these feelings as well as improve productivity by clearly communicating their leadership purpose and enabling employees to find theirs. When employees have a clear purpose, they're no longer concerned about fairness, they're concerned with doing their best work. Their mindset then shifts to the belief that work has the potential to make the lives of other employees or customers easier or better. When employees experience such a mindset shift, they embrace continual learning and growth. This leads to both a reduced sense of being overwhelmed as well as increased skillset and productivity.

Duncan: *In many work environments, everything is a priority so nothing is truly a priority. How can leaders identify and focus on the two or three priorities that provide the greatest leverage to sustainable success?*

Blane: The number one priority of most leaders is accomplishing their to-do list. For many they have become "a human doing" as opposed to a "human being." The good news about priority-setting is that increased effort isn't the answer. The answer is a ruthless determination to take one action every day that is aligned with their purpose and their promises.

How does a leader do this? One simple exercise is to create a to-be list. This is a list of the top three to five traits, attributes or values that are non-negotiable. This list helps prioritize the type of day a leader wants and directs their energies beyond their ever-expanding list of priorities on their to-do list. Every leader has a finite amount of time and resources. It's only by crafting the type of day a leader wants to create that they can prioritize their day and take action to create it.

Duncan: *What role does praising play in effective leadership, and what are the key ingredients?*

Blane: Praising is rooted in one essential leadership imperative. Praising builds the confidence employees have in themselves as well as in you as a leader worthy of being followed. Praising also encourages experimentation, risk-taking, and learning while also infusing hope and optimism into the workplace.

Praising becomes invaluable when it comes to enabling employees to flourish. The three ingredients of effective praising are: be sincere, be timely, be specific.

Praise must be sincere. Praise that is mechanical, obligatory, and/or delivered in a rote manner is seen as artificial and contrived, and fosters a relationship gap that undermines giving full effort to performance.

Praise must be timely. The most potent form of praise is the type that's delivered in real time. Catching employees doing something noteworthy and commenting on it immediately raises the well-being not only of the person receiving the praise, but creates a culture in which appreciation and continued growth become strategic assets.

Praise must also be specific. Generalized praise such as, "Good job!" pales in comparison to specific praise such as, "Your project management work on the Carson project was incredibly helpful. You lived out our strategic goal of improving our customer experience and let the client feel confident and at ease with your performance. They said they loved working with us. That was really good work."

Personal application:

- Be honest with yourself. Do you ever have a JDTM (Just Doing the Minimum) mindset? If so, what seems to trigger it? What can you do to replace that mindset with one that's more purpose-driven?

- In addition to your typical daily to-do list, what would (should) you put on your daily to-be list?

- What could be the result if you faithfully pursue each day's to-be list?

7

Your Brain Has a Mind of Its Own

Commentary: Rodger Dean Duncan

What you'll learn: You can make the best use of your brain by challenging your own stories.

At one time or another, most of us have claimed that our emotions—our feelings—are imposed on us, that we have no control. Admit it, you've probably said something like "He makes me so mad!"

The reality, tough though it may be to swallow, is that nobody can *make* us be mad, or glad, or sad, or anything else. We *choose* our feelings based on the stories we tell ourselves. Then our feelings lead to actions that produce results. If we don't like our results we can challenge our own thinking, because what we *think* is what launches us on our path to action that produces our results.

At first blush, this idea may come across as a touchy-feely mind game. It's not. The ability to improve our results by challenging our own thinking is one of the most powerful skills we can develop. It can unlock our true potential by freeing us from the constraints of the stories we often tell ourselves.

Let's see how this can work.

Your brain has a mind of its own. No kidding. On its own accord, the brain tends to act more out of self-preservation than out of rationality. We have a natural tendency to tell ourselves stories that justify what we're doing or failing to do. We have a natural tendency to allow our stories to masquerade as facts. We have a natural tendency to seek information that reinforces our view and to filter out or ignore information that contradicts our view.

When we're not careful, some of us can jump to conclusions faster than an Olympian can do a back flip. This isn't a character flaw, it's just part of being human. But these natural tendencies can be crippling. The good news is that we can teach ourselves a new set of behaviors that serve us better.

Here's an approach to challenging our own conclusions that I've discovered to be helpful. I've given it a name: FIND-IT, which stands for **F**ocus, **I**nquire, **N**otice, **D**iscern – **I**ntegrate, **T**ranslate.

First, let's examine the nuances of each of these action verbs.

To **F**ocus is to clarify, to concentrate, to define more carefully.

To **I**nquire is to investigate, to seek information by questioning. Effective inquiry requires an openness, a willingness to discover and accept information that differs from our first impressions or pre-conceived notions. Appreciative inquiry involves searching for solutions or explanations that may already exist and looking for the good and reasonable. That's not to suggest that we wear blinders that prevent our seeing what's dangerous or harmful. It's to suggest that we honestly consider the possibility of bright sunshine obscured by the dark clouds.

To **N**otice is to pay mindful attention to details, to become more aware of the individual parts that comprise the whole. I recall an art gallery that I visited with my grandchildren. A major exhibit featured the playful work of Walter Wick, the photographer whose *I SPY* and *Can You See What I See* books for children are longtime bestsellers. With careful examination, I was able to notice things in Wick's work that were completely missed in my initial, cursory look. In some situations there may be less than meets the eye. In others, there is definitely more than meets the eye. The only way to know is to notice mindfully.

To **D**iscern is to distinguish, to recognize as distinct or different. True discernment also involves wisdom. Egyptian novelist Naguib Mahfouz may have said it best: "You can tell whether a man is clever by his answers. You can tell whether a man is wise by his questions." In addition to its spiritual components, discernment is an outgrowth of honest inquiry and mindful noticing.

To **I**ntegrate involves incorporating parts into a whole, giving fair consideration to the possible interdependency of the individual pieces. A related word is *integral,* which denotes something that is necessary to complete the whole. Another related word is *integrity,* which denotes a state of being that's whole or complete, and, of course, soundness of moral character. All of these are essential to behavior that produces the best results.

To **T**ranslate is to change something's form, nature, or condition or to explain it in terms that are more easily understood and more appropriately dealt with.

To illustrate the utility of the FIND-IT model, let's consider my friend Stephen Covey's classic story of his experience on a subway. At one station stop a man stepped onto the subway along with several children. The man sat down, stared blankly at the floor, the train lurched forward, and the children went nuts. They pushed and shoved each other, wrestled over sitting space, and generally made a loud nuisance of themselves. One little boy, barely able to toddle, tripped over the feet of other passengers and seemed oblivious to the possible danger. Stephen found himself irritated with the man. His conclusion was that the man was rude and uncaring and simply wouldn't be bothered with managing his unruly children. So Stephen stepped across the aisle, sat down beside the man, and asked a couple of simple questions:

"Sir, are these your children?"

"Oh, yes they are."

"They seem anxious about something. Are you concerned that this littlest guy might get hurt in the crowd?"

Inside, Stephen was frankly annoyed by the children's behavior. Most of all he was annoyed by the man's apparent indifference to the situation. But then he got a response that changed everything.

"Oh, yeah, I realize the children are out of hand. You see, we just left the hospital. My wife has been gravely ill for several weeks. She died about an hour ago. I've told the children that their mother is gone and I'm afraid they're kind of in shock. I certainly am. I don't know how I'm going to live without my wife."

With that fresh insight, Stephen's paradigm—his "story" or frame of reference—changed instantly. Instead of viewing the man as rude and uncaring, he now saw him for what he was—a fellow human swallowed by grief and shock. And when Stephen's viewpoint changed, his behavior changed. His urge to judge and lecture was replaced by the urge to comfort and help. He offered to cancel his appointments and help the man, a total stranger who was suddenly humanized by more complete—and more accurate—information.

When we sincerely **F**ocus on a situation, we begin to see things that were not at first apparent.

When we respectfully **I**nquire—not for the purpose of playing "gotcha" but rather for the purpose of discovering possibilities we had not considered—we are often surprised by what we learn.

When we mindfully **N**otice the details of a situation we begin to see and appreciate the individual pixels that comprise the landscape.

When we carefully **D**iscern what's going on in a situation, we honestly distinguish between the facts (verifiable data) and our assumptions (the unsubstantiated stories we tell ourselves).

When we **I**ntegrate what we've noticed and discerned, we're well on our path to appropriate and useful conclusions, decisions, and behaviors.

Finally, we're able to **T**ranslate it all in a way that leads us to productive outcomes.

The next time you're struggling for a useful approach to a situation—as a leader, as a parent, as an employee, as a friend—do yourself and others a favor. FIND-IT.

Personal application:

- Under what circumstances are you sometimes tempted to abdicate responsibility for your emotions?

- How can you use the FIND-IT approach in your personal life?

- How can you use the FIND-IT approach in a professional environment?

8

Are You Headed Down a Negative Path? Why Mental Maps Matter

Expert: Robert Quinn, university professor, leadership coach, author

What you'll learn: A careful examination of our mental maps can help us navigate the complexities of organizational life.

"Once you replace negative thoughts with positive ones," said the great philosopher Willie Nelson, "you'll start having positive results."

Hardly anyone argues against being positive. But much of the rah-rah talk out there comes across as intellectual pablum.

Not so with the vitamin-enriched insights of Robert E. Quinn in his book *The Positive Organization: Breaking Free from Conventional Cultures, Constraints, and Beliefs.*

Where many writers in the business genre are adept at articulating worthy aspirations about being positive at work, Quinn focuses on translating the aspirations into specific and practical organizational actions. With compelling case studies from path-breaking companies where he's consulted, he provides real world guidance in the "how to."

If you're a leader in any kind of organization, or even if you're still learning how to be an effective follower, Bob Quinn's advice can help you and your colleagues flourish in an atmosphere of unified purpose.

Rodger Dean Duncan: *There's no doubt that people's mental maps influence their approach to and their beliefs about organizational culture. You identify three common viewpoints: the Discounters, the Skeptics, and the Believers. Can you differentiate between these viewpoints and comment on the advantage one may have over the others?*

Robert E. Quinn: If one finds a treasure map in a bottle, it would be wise to be skeptical. The positive mental map specifies the way to positive change and increased effectiveness. Yet it violates conventional assumptions. It's natural to discount it or to be skeptical. People cannot recreate their organization unless they fully believe in their desired future and are willing to move forward through adversity to create it. The job of a change leader is to create faith and belief. In the meantime, discounters and skeptics are imprisoned by they own sound logic. To become free requires a shift from fear to confidence in an emerging future.

Duncan: *What successful approaches have you found to help people challenge their beliefs and elevate their aspirations?*

Quinn: Commitment to a higher purpose, authentic communication, empathy, and co-creation. Organizational excellence is an emergent phenomenon. Effective change leaders are not experts with a plan. They are facilitators with a vision.

Duncan: *Many organizations seem to have cultures that disempower or discourage people. What are some good ways to identify systems and practices that produce such (usually) unintended consequences?*

Quinn: The conventional assumptions that we all make from the time we can talk are based on fear and the need to be in control. In left-brain analysis of any problem, the subject of the analysis is an object. When we see people as problems, we objectify them. Our most basic assumptions about organizations and authority are inherently disempowering.

Duncan: *When cultural constraints are identified, how do you persuade senior leaders—who may inadvertently be part of the problem—to make needed changes?*

Quinn: The boss is always part of the problem. That's why consultants so often fail. They are brought in by the boss who thinks he or she wants the problem solved. Once the problem is fully understood, the consultant sees that the boss is part of the problem, but the self-interested consultant fears confronting the issue because the consultant is working for money, not the good of the system.

The question itself is conventional. It assumes rational persuasion is the key to transformation. It is not. Senior leaders are terrified but have to act as if they are not. Rational persuasion simply makes them more defensive. A transformative leader leads the boss the same way he or she leads subordinates: by clarifying purpose, increasing integrity, empathy and humility and then engaging in difficult conversations because he or she is committed to the common good.

Duncan: *You say it's important for a leader to be culturally "bilingual."*

For example, a leader can benefit from a conventional mental map that depicts the organization as a pyramid, a hierarchy of positions ... while simultaneously using a mental map that depicts the organization as a network of relationships. How does such a dual viewpoint guide leaders to better choices and actions, and how can a leader develop this ability?

Quinn: A novice looks for simplicity in complexity. An expert understands complexity but confuses the novice. A master brings the simplicity from the other side of complexity to the novice. An expert in finance or some other discipline uses logic to create value. But as they go up the system, their logic begins to fail and they destroy value. They do not know the simplicity from the other side of complexity. Usually in crisis the expert crumbles and the master emerges. The master is bilingual.

Duncan: *What can leaders do to "think about the whole" rather than cling to the narrow lens of their own background or discipline?*

Quinn: When we think we are in charge, we look down and see the parts. We see silos. We see individuals. This is the logic of most managers. So they can never optimize the potential in the system. When we look up and see the whole, it is bigger than we are. It is complex and dynamic. The only way to move the whole is to connect it to a higher purpose and integrate the differentiated parts. That gives rise to emergence and the unfolding of collective intelligence.

Duncan: *You write that many leaders are slaves to problem solving and that they should focus instead on "high purpose." What does that mean in the real world of real work?*

Quinn: Even the senior most leaders got to where they are by being great problem solvers. Transactional problem solving is at the heart of the managerial identity. Transformative purpose finding simply does not make sense to the addicted problem solver. Yet, it is not until we can discover, articulate and animate purpose that we ever move the whole. In the real world of work, purpose finding is what leaders do.

Duncan: *Much of the work in organizations involves conversations, face-to-face interactions between people. What gets in the way of truly productive conversations and how can people get better at this most basic skill?*

Quinn: I spend a lot of time putting executives into authentic conversations. They need me because they cannot do it themselves. What gets in the way is that it is natural to be "on-stage." In organizations, which are full of fear, our every conversation is adapted to the current political context. People can get better at authentic conversations when they shift from a fearful focus on survival to a courageous focus on the collective good.

Duncan: *Someone once said that every organization is perfectly aligned to get the results it's getting. How can that viewpoint serve as a filter in assessing systems, processes, and behaviors that produce either negative or positive results?*

Quinn: Conventional logic says that the present is determined by the past. Social science shows that people are "path dependent." They do what cultural experience has trained them to do. They are prisoners of their own experience. So, we fail and we keep repeating what we are already doing, while we complain about failing. This is the definition of insanity and we are all insane. The positive mental model asks, "When is the present shaped by the future?" The answer is when we establish and fully commit to a purpose. At that moment we become a proactive influence in a reactive world. We become fully conscious and we move forward, learning in real time. We become a system of leadership.

Personal application:

- What can you do to help create faith and believe in bringing about needed change and/or improvement in your organization?

- How can you do a better job of "thinking about the whole" as you operate in your organization?

- How can you improve in your ability to hold "authentic conversations" with co-workers about performance issues?

Workplace Practices

"The best way to add value to yourself is by adding value to other people."

John Maxwell

9

How to Boost Your Value in the Workplace

Expert: Jodi Glickman, executive coach, author of *Great on the Job*

What you'll learn: Communication skills play a critical role in your work success, beginning with the first 30 seconds of the job interview.

With unemployment rates at record lows, some people may get lulled into complacency about their marketability. After all, they may reason, jobs are so plentiful it's easy to pick and choose among opportunities.

That shortsighted perspective can be deadly for their futures.

Regardless of the current state of the economy, it's always a good idea to regard every day as another chance to hone your skills and make your best practices even better.

That's the view of Jodi Glickman, an expert in training people how to be *Great on the Job.* In fact, that's the title of her bestselling book.

In addition to training, coaching, and consulting, Glickman has been a regular blogger for Harvard Business Review and has appeared on MSNBC. Her career advice has been featured in the *New York Times, USA Today, BusinessWeek, WSJ Finance, CNN Money, Woman's Day* and many other media outlets. She's a former Peace Corp volunteer (Southern Chile) turned investment banker (Goldman Sachs) turned communication expert. She earned her MBA at Cornell University.

I visited with Jodi about workplace issues that affect everyone in most every kind of job.

Rodger Dean Duncan: *What are the two or three most common communication mistakes in a business environment—and what advice do you offer for solving them.*

Jodi Glickman: The first one is failing to manage expectations. We make a lot of assumptions that people know what we're thinking, what we want a finished product to look like, when we want to see the final sales numbers. The antidote is explicit communication. If you give me an assignment and I have 20 other things on my plate, I should respond immediately and communicate to you when I'll be able to handle your request. This builds trust and demonstrates that you're on top of things. Let people know their needs are on your radar and that you'll follow up at a specific time.

If you're handing off work, clarify *your* expectations. Clearly communicate how you want the finished product to look and when you need to have it.

Mistake number two: failing to ask for help. Many people are afraid of looking dumb, so they set themselves up for failure because they don't ask for the resources and guidance they need to meet expectations. Asking for help doesn't mean saying, "I have no idea what to do." Asking for help means saying, "Okay, this is the way I understand it. Is this what you have in mind?" You may want to put together a plan of action, then get your manager's buy-in to ensure that you're moving in the right direction. An agreement on direction, project steps, and milestones can be helpful to all parties.

Mistake number three: failing to use face-to-face communication when it's needed. Many people use email as a crutch when they don't want to have a difficult conversation with someone or they don't feel comfortable delivering bad news. If you fail to address an issue head-on, there's a good chance it will blow up to become an even greater problem. Tone and tenor get lost in email. In business, most decisions don't get made via email. It's through face-to-face communication.

Duncan: *Why do some people seem to ignore—or resist—the need to get help with their relationships at work?*

Glickman: People tend to focus on technical skills. Technical and financial skills are sometimes easier to deal with because we can measure output. Relationship issues are often more difficult (though not impossible) to measure. The easy way is to simply ignore problems. If we promote people to management positions because they have good technical skills, and then just hope that they will automatically develop people skills, we're headed for trouble. Similarly, some people resist coaching with a comment like, "You know, I don't really need help. Things will take care of themselves." People often avoid confronting a colleague who genuinely needs help with relationships.

Self-awareness is one of the common denominators of great leaders. Leadership is not just drive, ambition, intelligence, or vision. It comes down to knowing what you're good at and knowing what you're not yet good at. Self-awareness enables you to capitalize on your strengths and outsource or compensate for your weaknesses and get better at those things in which you need improvement.

Duncan: *What tips can you offer on the best ways to give—and receive—feedback on the job?*

Glickman: The most important thing in giving feedback is to be specific. Don't just tell someone they need to get better. Offer specific examples and tips. Otherwise, you're giving frustration, not help. Be prepared to tell the person what you think he should do differently, or what he should stop doing, or what he should *start* doing. Jason Garrett, coach of the Dallas Cowboys, says the coaches he appreciated most in his playing days were those who were very explicit in telling him how he could improve.

We should not look at feedback as something to make us feel good or bad about ourselves. We should regard feedback as developmental. It's sometimes like medicine. It may not taste good, but it can help us get better. If I really care about becoming the best professional I can be, then I should welcome your constructive criticism.

People need to ask for feedback explicitly. You can't safely assume that people will automatically give you feedback. You should plant the seed in advance. You don't want to put anyone on the spot and say, "How did I do in that presentation?" Tell them in advance that you will ask for feedback. This enables them to be thinking about how they can offer feedback that will be helpful.

Duncan: *In today's super competitive environment, how can good communication skills help a person stand out from the crowd?*

Glickman: The reality is that when you meet someone, you're sizing them up within 30 seconds. That might not seem fair, but it's reality. You're either impressed by their poise and maturity and confidence, or you're not. And it all comes across in the way they're able to communicate to you in that first half minute.

Let's assume you're sharp and on the ball and have what it takes to back up a good first impression. Still, the only way you're going to get the job is to impress the potential employer that you have something valuable to offer. No matter how smart you are, if you can't talk it's very hard to compete for the best job.

Personal application:

- What can you do to improve the way you manage expectations— whether you're giving or receiving a work assignment?

- How can you improve the way you solicit—and receive—feedback on your performance?

- How can you do a better job of offering feedback to others?

10

Office Politics:
Tools for Taking Charge

Expert: Rob Fazio, advisor to C-suite executives and up-and-coming leaders, author of *Simple Is the New Smart*

What you'll learn: Some form of "politics" is inevitable in most any workplace. How you handle it can have a profound effect on your career (and your sanity).

The word politics, it's been said, is derived from the word "poly" meaning "many," and the word "ticks" meaning "blood sucking parasites."

Well, not really.

But regardless of its linguistic roots, politics can be tough. Including office politics.

Studies show that many people who claim dissatisfaction with their jobs are actually OK with the work itself. Their dissatisfaction is with relationships—with managers and/or co-workers.

A new book offers guidance on navigating the sometimes rough waters of office politics. It's titled *Simple Is the New Smart*. Its author, Rob Fazio, suggests how to build confidence and inspire yourself in the workplace.

Rodger Dean Duncan: *What's your advice on how to deal effectively with a bad boss or dysfunctional colleague?*

Rob Fazio: While someone who works for a difficult person may think there is no way out, there actually is. The first thing to know is that you always have a choice and should do everything you can to avoid getting "stuck" in a job or working for a boss who creates a dysfunctional environment. Sometimes when the smart thing to do is find a way out from underneath that boss or to find a new organization. While I know that's rarely an easy option, here are some tips.

Be your boss' boss. Alpha personalities sniff out fear and leverage it to their advantage. I worked with an executive who had a boss that would lose his composure, yell, and blame everyone else. What we worked on was not letting what his boss did or said throw him off his game. He got really good at doing the opposite of what his boss did in conversations. The more emotional his boss got, the less emotion my client demonstrated. The more the boss would focus on what went wrong or who was to blame, my client talked about what could be done going forward and what solutions were possible.

Know it's not personal, it's professional. A common mistake is to take dysfunction personally. It has nothing to do with you. It has to do with what's going on inside your boss's head. Often, ineffective bosses become magnifiers of the pressure they feel. The more you can realize that your boss is likely under a great deal of pressure and he or she isn't looking to do something negative to you, the better able you are to be empathetic and focus on seeing things from a different perspective. Keep reminding yourself it's about the job, not you. That will allow you to remain composed and focused on what you need to do, rather than how you feel.

Duncan: *Honest conversation, you say, is the best tool in dealing with behavior issues. Give us an example of a difficult situation and how you recommend using honest conversation to address it.*

Fazio: A banking client of mine was struggling with being elevated to co-head along with another colleague. The challenge was that my client felt she was getting put up against the other co-head, and only one of them could be successful. She was at a loss because she thought the only option she had was to win or lose as she and her colleague fought for "turf" and who would own which clients. Just like in any business some of their clients would naturally elevate each of their numbers. If one of the co-heads got stuck with non-performing clients, it would impact their success and upward mobility.

What I encouraged and coached my client to do was have an honest conversation with her colleague. She asked for a 1:1 meeting. She started with honesty. She shared her view that if the two of them didn't find a way to create a fair playing ground, the deck would be stacked against one of them. She proposed that rather than having their boss determine who serviced what clients, they should make those arrangements together and then speak to the boss as a united front. This was difficult because it was a risk to put on the table that there is a natural competition between the two of them. The other person could have decided not to go along with the plan and taken advantage of the situation. The outcome was that a stronger level of trust and transparency was created between the co-heads. Also, their boss respected the landscape of healthy competition they created.

Conversations are the most important tool for success. We all have conversations that we avoid because they're uncomfortable. You can go into a conversation with both strength and vulnerability. Transparency and honesty will get you further in the long run. If someone burns you, you know where they stand and can protect yourself for the future.

Duncan: *Stress can be a killer (literally). What are the similarities between the stress felt by a professional athlete and the stress felt by a business executive? And how similar is the advice you offer to deal with it?*

Fazio: Both athletes and executives face the pressure of winning by maintaining edge, energy, and focus while faced with countless distractions. We've learned from sport psychology that there's a sweet spot where there is enough pressure to help us perform, but not so much pressure that is makes us melt down. As you gain experience, skills, and confidence you're better able to handle pressure and perform.

The advice is the same whether you're a professional athlete or, what I call, a "business athlete." First, *see it.* Realize that whether you are taking the game-winning shot or having a challenging conversation with a colleague, it's a performance. As with all performances, you need to envision ahead of time how you want it to go.

Second, *say it.* The most focused athletes are able to focus when it counts. One way to do this is to have a trigger word that gets you ready to perform. The best way to come up with a trigger word is to think of a time you were your most confident and at your best. What word is associated with that moment?

Third, *start it.* In football, coaches often say that, after the first snap, the nerves go away and your skills take over. Rehearse how you want to start your performance and what messages you want to get across. Then go for it and get in the game. Stress declines after we build our skills and experiences.

The advice ends up being similar in that for both you need to have a strong level of psychological swagger. If you believe in yourself, you create a foundation from which you can focus on what you can control, which is your mindset. This leads to success, no matter if you're in an office building or on the playing field.

Duncan: *You suggest that listening is bad for your health. Please elaborate.*

Fazio: Listening to negative messages can limit us mentally and physically. On the physical side there's a strong connection between negative self-talk and lowering our immune systems. There's evidence suggesting that self-talk can impact our health and actually change our brains. According to Stanford University neurology professor Robert Sapolsky, a half hour of complaining every day physically damages a person's brain. This goes for both the listener and the complainer, as exposure to negativity peels back neurons in the hippocampus. That's the part of the brain used for problem solving and cognitive function.

In addition, according to the Mayo Clinic, listening to negative self-talk, whether from yourself or others, can contribute to poor cardiovascular and gut health. On the mental/emotional side, negative self-talk and complaining can contribute to high levels of stress and even depression, which lead to poor bodily health.

My focus is mastering what only you can master: what you tell yourself. The downside of being a rookie at listening is that you listen and internalize everything from anyone you view as more powerful than you. The result is listening to the wrong things from the wrong people and internalizing the messages that become the ties that hold you down. If you listen to the wrong messages it will limit your progress toward your success and worse, diminish your drive.

Personal application:

- What steps can you take to ensure that *you* are not somehow contributing to dysfunctional behavior in the workplace?

- What situations in your workplace could benefit from honest conversation? How can you best prepare to have such conversation(s)?

- What are the sources of negativity that you should learn to ignore?

11

Workplace Matters:
How to Make It Great

Expert: Michael Bush, author, CEO of Great Place to Work for All

What you'll learn: The standard for what constitutes a "great" workplace is changing. You can be part of the wave.

Everyone wants a great workplace. An environment where the work is both interesting and challenging. Where people collaborate to promote the worthy cause of terrific products or make-a-difference services. Where careers blossom and the bottom line thrives.

For more than two decades, Great Place to Work has produced annual lists of the 100 Best Companies to Work For. The lists are anything but arbitrary. They're based on rigorous standards backed up by uncompromising research.

By now you know some of the players: companies like Adobe, Salesforce, Mercedes-Benz, Whole Foods, Marriott, American Express, Hyatt, Mars, Aflac, Nordstrom, FedEx. These and others have earned a coveted spot in the workplace hall of fame.

But as the song lyric says, the times they are a changin'.

The implication of change in the modern workplace is detailed in *A Great Place to Work for All* by Michael Bush, CEO of the Great Place to Work organization. He reveals the essential values and behaviors that every organization must follow to thrive in the future.

Rodger Dean Duncan: *You begin your book by saying that what was good enough to be "great" 10 or 20 years ago is not good enough now. What has changed?*

Michael Bush: It's no longer good enough to have a great experience for just some of your people.

When I came on as CEO, I knew people at our 100 Best Companies who weren't having a great experience. So we dug into our data. We found that even at the best, many people were being left out. They were experiencing a different organization than their colleagues.

We recognized the problem and took an approach to make sure that all people—women, people of color, of different nationalities, of different job levels—worked in a positive environment where they can thrive.

We raised the bar so that a company has to be consistently great. It has to be great not just for some, but for all. We did this not just because it's the right thing to do. But because when a company is a great place to work for all, it brings out the best in everyone. That's better for business.

Duncan: *After decades of surveying tens of millions of workers in scores of industries, your organization added "maximizing human potential" to your measurement standards. What precipitated that change?*

Bush: For one thing, we needed to take stock of the new economic landscape. This is a business climate defined by speed, social technologies and people expecting values besides value. For people to give your organization all of their potential they want respect, fairness, and some form of equity in return. If they aren't getting these things the organization is getting a suboptimal return. This is the case in the majority of the companies we survey. The organizations that are maximizing this potential grow revenue four times faster than the companies that get less of this potential.

Secondly, we listened to our clients and the Best Workplaces we work with. They made this point too. Cisco's executive chairman, John Chambers, for example, says the digital revolution requires companies to rely ever more on those on the front line. "Decisions will be made much further down in the organization at a fast pace," he told us.

Finally, maximizing human potential is great all around. When all employees are at their best at work, it's better for businesses, better for people and better for the world.

Duncan: *There's no doubt that trust fuels performance. What kind of behaviors build and maintain trust in the workplace?*

Bush: Leaders are key. From executives down to front-line managers, leaders need to demonstrate respect, credibility and fairness to employees. Those are the building blocks of trust. Leaders increase trust every time they listen carefully to employees, live up to their word and treat all people in an even-handed way. The very best leaders—what we call For All Leaders—also cultivate strong bonds with their teams, connect everyone to the mission of the organization, and spotlight team members' successes.

Another trust-building behavior is providing everyone with opportunities to innovate. A great example is software company Adobe and its

"Kickboxes." These "personal innovation kits" are boxes with guidance inside on developing new ideas, a Starbucks gift card and $1,000 in seed money. Any employee can get one—no questions asked. About 2,000 Kickboxes have been given out in recent years, leading to new products and internal process improvements. Opportunities to innovate boost your business and shows employees you trust them to do great things.

Duncan: *In companies that struggle with negative public relations issues—Uber and Facebook come to mind—what can leaders do to revitalize the confidence of employees?*

Bush: They can start by building credibility and respect by sharing the truth of the problem transparently. They can listen to employees' reactions and possible solutions. They can include these perspectives as a plan is built for the future. And they can uphold values, even when that's tough.

One example is the way health care system Texas Health Resources handled an Ebola scare several years ago. The hospital involved suffered a drop in patient visits because of public fears of the disease, but Texas Health CEO Barclay Berdan refused to lay off employees. The organization lived up to its "Individuals Caring for Individuals, Together" promise, and revenue recovered by the end of the year.

Duncan: *Not surprisingly, your research shows that work experience tends to be more positive at higher levels in organizations. What can be done to boost work satisfaction at lower levels?*

Bush: Respect them. The best way to do so doesn't cost you any money and in fact will increase your revenue: give everyone chances to come up with new and better products, services and processes. Create what we call an "Innovation By All" culture, which taps into the human desire to be creative, to contribute. Our research shows that companies that are most inclusive in their innovation activities grow revenue 5.5 times faster than companies that have the least "By All" culture of innovation.

I mentioned Adobe's Kickbox program earlier. Another example is hospitality giant Hilton. Hilton has a "Make it Right" mantra, which encourages everyone at all levels to take the initiative to solve problems. Front line workers at Hilton don't just make it right, they make it better. One housekeeper told us she learned while cleaning a room that a couple was celebrating their anniversary. So she got room service to give them a bottle of wine as a gift. That makes for five-star service and a happy employee.

Duncan: *What should a "For All" organization look for when recruiting new employees?*

Bush: First, aim to hire a workforce that reflects the make-up of your community. You can't get the benefits of For All culture—which includes the proven advantages of diverse perspectives—if you don't have "All" kinds of people there in the first place.

Also, look for people who want to learn, who are open to different perspectives. Great Places to Work For All are dynamic, so employees can expect their roles and responsibilities to change over time. And they need to be comfortable being uncomfortable at times. They must be willing to be challenged by people who have different viewpoints.

Finally, big egos aren't a positive. You're looking for people who are driven by a bigger purpose and ready to collaborate to achieve it.

Duncan: *In light of your research findings, what kind of questions should today's job applicants be asking their prospective employers?*

Bush: Do they respect employees enough to share information and decision-making? Do they show a commitment to For All by having a diverse set of people in leadership roles? Have they made some tough decisions to stand by their values? Can they tell a story of letting go a top performer who was a cancer on the culture?

Software company Workday did just that. Their CEO, Aneel Bhusri, looked at the data showing that one his lieutenants wasn't creating the collegial atmosphere the company expects. By ousting this leader, Bhusri showed For All Leadership. I'd ask for a story like this.

Personal application:

- What role can you play in making your job environment a great place to work?

- Regardless of your title or role, what can you do to build trust in your organization?

- Again, regardless of your title or role, what can you do to help others in your organization have a better work experience?

12

How to Develop Your People

Expert: Erika Andersen, consultant to companies ranging from Citi-Group to Taco Bell, author of *Leading So People Will Follow*

What you'll learn: Leadership has more in common with gardening than you might suspect.

Erika Andersen is an accomplished author, consultant, and coach. But what really sets her apart is her insistence on sustainability. She's not interested in a simple consulting gig. She wants to make a measurable, long-term difference in people's performance (and lives).

Follow through and reinforcement are hallmarks of Erika's work in organizational development and collaborative learning. Erika's clients range from MTV Networks and NBC Universal to CitiGroup and Taco Bell. Her books include *Growing Great Employees: Turning Ordinary People into Extraordinary Performers; Being Strategic: Plan for Success, Out-think Your Competitors;* and *Leading So People Will Follow.* I really like Erika. I trust her message and approach. Hers is definitely a voice worth hearing.

Rodger Dean Duncan: *You've sometimes used the metaphor of a gardener in discussing the work of managers and leaders. Can you elaborate on that?*

Erika Andersen: I find gardening a really useful metaphor for people management, both in the specifics and in the core premise. Here's what I mean: The essential truth about gardening is that you can't *make* plants grow. You can get a plant that's well-suited to the conditions you have in your garden and the role in the garden you want it to play, and you can provide the support (water, nutrients, pruning, etc.) that will best help it survive and thrive. But after that, it's up to the plant.

In the same way, managers can make sure they get people who are best-suited to their organizations, and best able to play the role they want them to play, and provide them with the necessary support (listening, clear agreements, feedback, coaching)—but after that, it's up to them. You can't *make* employees grow and thrive; all you can do is create the optimal conditions and provide consistent support. But if you do that (in either gardening or managing), you're most likely to get great results.

Duncan: *What do you see as some of the most common barriers to organizational performance?*

Andersen: Poor leadership. Most of the other barriers (a flawed business model, insufficient operating capital, lack of needed talent, over- or under-engineered systems, poor communication) come back, in the end, to poor leadership. People need and deserve leaders who are far-sighted, passionate, courageous, wise, generous and trustworthy. That is, leaders who articulate and then fully engage them in moving toward a clear and attainable vision (far-sighted); who commit honestly and deeply to ideas and initiatives about which they feel strongly (passionate); who make tough, necessary choices and take full responsibility for those choices (courageous); who reflect deeply to make informed decisions and learn from mistakes and successes (wise); who assume positive intent and support their people's success (generous); and who keep their word and deliver on their promises (trustworthy).

When an organization doesn't have leaders with most of these attributes—especially at the top, but ideally at all levels of leadership—it's virtually impossible to succeed long-term.

Duncan: *A lot of business people use the terms strategy and tactics interchangeably. How do you draw a distinction between the two?*

Andersen: Yes, and I'm thrilled that you asked! Helping people understand these two things, so they can use them as the powerful tools they are, is an important aspect of the work we do with clients.

We define being strategic as *consistently making those core directional choices that will best move you toward your hoped-for future*. Strategies are those *core directional choices*. Another way to think of a strategy is as a statement of intention, a way to state, simply and clearly: "This is a path we intend to take to achieve our vision." Tactics are the 'bricks in the path'—the specific actions you'll need to take to implement your strategy.

Here's an example from a recent client session with the senior team of an entertainment company. One of the strategies they agreed upon to achieve their vision was *Foster an environment that inspires creative thinking and pride of ownership*—a clear statement of intention about this aspect of their business. Two of the tactics they came up with to execute this strategy: "Establish a monthly cross-departmental meeting to focus on an agreed upon, long-lead topic. At least one idea pursued from each meeting," and "Recommend and execute feasible ways to make the physical environment supportive of creative thinking/ pride of ownership." Both great examples of specific, high-leverage actions to take in order to implement that strategy.

Duncan: *Many change efforts seem to create a "culture backlash." What are some ways to manage—or avoid—that kind of resistance?*

Andersen: When change efforts don't work (which is, sadly, more often than not) it's generally because senior management tries to mandate the change without really engaging people or acknowledging the impact it will have on them. You cover this topic beautifully in your book *CHANGE-friendly LEADERSHIP*, and our approach is very much aligned with yours.

When we work with clients to shift their culture, we share with them that people will generally only change their behavior if the new behavior *seems to them* to be easy, rewarding and normal. *Easy* means they understand how to do it, feel competent to do it, don't see any organizational impediments to do doing it—and in fact believe the organization will support them if they do. *Rewarding* means they see how it will give them something(s) they value. *Normal* means they believe it's something that others like them are willing and able to do, and that it's something that people whom they admire and respect do. If you make it clear to people what the change will entail, in terms of them behaving differently, and then work with them to make sure those changes are easy, rewarding, and normal *for them*—any "cultural backlash" tends to dissipate.

Duncan: *What have you found to be the best ways to help people retain and productively use the learning they acquire in training?*

Andersen: Some of what I've noted above applies here, too: before we do management or leadership training in a client company, we help them make sure that the new behaviors will be both easy and normal to do in the organization, once learned. During the training, we focus with the participants on understanding how and why it will be rewarding for them to behave in these new ways, and make the skills as easy as possible to learn and practice.

Finally, after the training, we help build in reinforcement—primarily from making sure there are immediate opportunities to practice the skills, but also through e-learning, check-ins with their manager and/ or learning partners, and follow-up training sessions. The main focus needs to be getting people to a point, as quickly as possible, where they're seeing that the new behavior is working better for them than their previous approach. That's when real growth happens.

Personal Application:

- How can you use the gardening metaphor to help guide your work in developing yourself and others?

- What steps can you take to ensure that people in your organization understand the difference between strategy and tactics?

- After you've received any kind of training, how do you reinforce what you've learned (through repetition, practice, etc.)?

Behaviors

"To change a habit, make
a conscious decision.
Then act out the
new behavior."

Maxwell Maltz

13

You Don't Need a Title to Be a Leader

Expert: Mark Sanborn, leadership coach, bestselling author of *The Fred Factor, Encore Effect, The Potential Principle* and other books.

What you'll learn: You are likely surrounded by opportunities to improve your skills and demonstrate your value.

Being a long-time student of leadership, I've naturally heard a lot of pithy quotes about the subject. One of my favorites is from Margaret Thatcher: "Being a leader is like being a lady. If you have to remind people you are, you aren't."

Well said, Madame Prime Minister!

And another, by John Quincy Adams: "If your actions inspire others to dream more, learn more, do more, and become more, you are a leader."

I explored this and related issues with Mark Sanborn. He's president of Sanborn & Associates, an idea studio dedicated to developing leaders in business and in life. A graduate of Ohio State University, Mark is an international bestselling author and a noted authority on leadership, team building, customer service, and change. His many books include *The Fred Factor* and *You Don't Need a Title to Be a Leader*.

Rodger Dean Duncan: *I often tell people that you don't need a title to be a leader, and you wrote an entire book by that name. What are the three most important keys to exerting positive influence with others when you have no "position power" or authority?*

Mark Sanborn: If I ever re-title the book, I'll call it *You Don't Need a Title to Be a Leader But If You Do It Right a Title Won't Mess You Up.* I've got nothing against titles *per se*, but they're often misunderstood. Skills and results make you a leader. Titles should confirm leadership but they can never bestow it.

I'd begin by asking, "Why do you want to lead? What difference do you want to make?" Leadership has become trendy and many want to be "leaders" but don't necessarily have compelling reasons. Leadership should be borne out of a desire to contribute rather than simply achieve. Leadership done right benefits both the leader and the greater good: followers, the organization, and/or the community. Know why you want to lead because without compelling reasons, you probably won't be able to pay the cost of developing your leadership abilities and maintain your commitment in the face of challenges.

Next, look for opportunities to lead. Don't wait for someone to bring them to you. What needs to be done at your organization? What problems need solutions? What opportunities could be seized? What could be improved? Initiative is a pre-requisite to effective influence. Look around. Pay attention. Get involved.

Finally, be willing to do what others aren't. Work a little harder and smarter, prepare a little more, and study a little more deeply. If you're asked to do something (lead a project or head a task force), consider it an opportunity to improve your leadership abilities and deliver results that will showcase your abilities and prove you are a leader.

Duncan: *This is a time when a lot of people feel disconnected from the workplace. What can leaders do to encourage their people to take more personal responsibility for the organization's success?*

Sanborn: First, be clear on what those you lead are responsible for. Followers need clear focus on what they're accountable for doing and the kind of results they're expected to consistently achieve.

Second, consider the "fit" between the person and the task. One nuance of good leadership is matching not just the right people to the right job, but the best person to a particular job. "Best" is usually the person with the skills and interest, not just the ability to do the work.

Third, don't overlook a discussion of consequences. People are accountable to the degree they feel they are going to experience a benefit or avoid a negative. If not taking responsibility has the same outcome as taking responsibility, why bother?

Duncan: *Over the past couple of decades the economy has had some ups and downs. When it's down, many people feel discouraged about their prospects for the future. What advice do you give anyone facing adversity?*

Sanborn: In tough times you need both information and inspiration. Information is essential to understand what's going on. Some say, "Don't read the news. It's only negative." That is shortsighted advice. If there is news of an upcoming storm you need to know so you can prepare. Ignoring it won't make the storm go away. We all need to face reality.

We also need to be inspired by focusing on what we can do to respond successfully. Neuroscience has shown that we aren't just happy because we are successful, but we're successful because we're happy. Focusing more on the good than the bad, focusing on what we have rather than what we don't have – these predispose us to doing better and achieving our goals.

I like to offer people hope, which I define as having something new to try and being willing to try it. There is no hopeless situation if you can find something different to try and you are willing to act on the idea. Keep searching for new solutions and don't let lack of past success in dealing with a problem trick you into thinking there's nothing you can do.

Duncan: *Even in times when employment can be very fragile, many people do only enough to "just get by." What can a good leader do to inspire such people to perform better?*

Sanborn: Great leaders help people have a larger vision of themselves. Leaders look for the potential in followers that followers often don't recognize in themselves.

Expect more from those you lead and you'll get more. Don't be delusional and expect the impossible or you run the risk of demoralizing those you lead. And know that when you expect more from others you won't always get it, but you will get more from them than you would have gotten otherwise.

Connect behavior with outcomes. Show followers evidence of how their work impacts others, like customers and colleagues. Create a connection between what they do and the kind of difference they make.

Duncan: *Some politicians don't seem to understand that being a good campaigner does not necessarily translate into being an effective leader. What leadership advice would you give people who run for public office?*

Sanborn: The political process is the best and worst example of what leadership should be. Done right it shows how influence, understanding the process, creating support and serving constituents can work. Done wrong it becomes a debacle of empty promises and disappointed voters.

I'll summarize what I think all leaders, and those running for public office, should constantly remind themselves: Leaders don't just tell a better story; leaders make the story better.

Good communication skills are a tool of leadership, not an outcome. Nobody likes spin, hype and exaggeration. We all want leaders who can tell us what they'll achieve and then do it. Campaigning has little to do with leadership. Governing after the election is where a person's leadership is proved or disproved. I believe it was Mario Cuomo who said you campaign in poetry but you govern in prose. He knew the difference between the rhetoric of the campaign and the results expected of the elected.

Politicians, like all of us, should never write checks with their mouths that their bodies can't cash. The words are familiar but the strategy is still rock solid: under-promise and over-deliver.

Personal application:

- How can you help foster an atmosphere of personal accountability in your workplace?

- What can you do to take more responsibility for your own success?

- If you overheard some of your workmates talking about you, what would you hope to hear them say?

14

Why 'Etiquette' is So Much More Than Just Saying Please

Expert: Rosanne Thomas, "professional presence" consultant, author of *Excuse Me: The Survival Guide to Modern Business Etiquette*

What you'll learn: The "rules" of etiquette seem to vary by generation, gender, social background and other factors. It's a challenging road to navigate. But you can do it.

It's been said that the test of good manners is the ability to put up pleasantly with bad ones. But in a world where in-your-face behavior is sometimes mistaken as a strength, it's often hard to understand the rules of etiquette.

Etiquette. It's a fussy word that almost defies definition. I grew up at a time when I'd get extra homework if I dared say "Yeah" to a teacher rather than "Yes, sir." Men stood when a lady entered the room. I never referred to my parents' friends by their first names. I asked to be excused before leaving the dinner table.

Those "Leave It to Beaver" days seem very distant now. But I still want to behave in ways that show respect for others without coming across as an antique from another era.

I'm apparently not alone. And thanks to a fine book by "professional presence" consultant Rosanne Thomas, there's guidance on everything from first impression management to social media savvy. The book is *Excuse Me: The Survival Guide to Modern Business Etiquette.*

I talked with Thomas to explore some of the more pressing "etiquette" concerns borne of blended generations, mixed cultures, omnipresent technology, and gender issues. Whether you're a novice or an experienced professional, her advice is well worth considering.

Rodger Dean Duncan: *Most people would agree that a respectful workplace is a more pleasant workplace. What are some of the measurable bottom-line advantages that accrue to organizations that insist on respect and civility?*

Rosanne Thomas: Unreturned phone calls, condescending remarks, public reprimands, angry emails—just some of the countless ways in which incivility rears its head—come at an enormous cost to employers.

Unlike bullying, which is a coordinated, persistent effort to cause someone physical or emotional harm, incivility is often played down as relatively harmless. In fact, it's estimated that workplace incivility costs companies an average of $14,000 in lost productivity *per employee, per year*. Organizations also face exposure to increased legal, medical, and hiring costs because of incivility.

And it's contagious. Employees subjected to incivility often act in the same manner toward coworkers and customers, resulting in fractious relationships and increased customer service issues. Incivility also negatively affects co-workers who witness it, causing them stress and job insecurity. Conversely, organizations that insist on respect and civility see teamwork fostered, morale improved, problems solved, and productivity increased. Their reputations are burnished, enabling them to recruit the best and the brightest talent. An enhanced bottom-line is virtually inevitable, and happy shareholders are the ultimate result.

Duncan: *You rightfully say the foundation of civility is respect, which is the outward expression of esteem or deference. Yet social media, political discourse, the diatribes on talk shows and virtually every other public example of human interaction is rife with disrespect and put-downs. With that as a backdrop, what can an organization do to promote a culture of civility and respect?*

Thomas: An organization can remember that incivility as a model for life or work is unsustainable. It threatens the well-being and existence of what we need most in order to survive: other people.

The abuse of power—incivility at its core—works only as long as individuals are captive audiences. Once choice is restored—where to work, what establishments to patronize, with whom to associate—incivility, along with the individuals and organizations that tolerate it, will be rejected. Savvy organizations know this. And they clearly communicate their Codes of Conduct. They invest in civility training to reinforce best behaviors. They hire for attitude over experience, recognizing it's much easier to teach technical skills than it is to instill qualities of empathy and consideration. They provide safe channels for the reporting of disrespect, and when it's reported they take swift and appropriate action.

Duncan: *The culture of any organization is shaped by the worst behavior the leader is willing to tolerate. What can people do when the leader tolerates behavior that violates the organization's professed standards?*

Thomas: When a leader tolerates or engages in bad behavior, especially when it runs counter to the organization's avowed standards, credibility is lost. A confused and demoralized staff is left wondering exactly what is expected of them. Is it really okay to cut others off in the middle of sentences, openly criticize their intelligence and abilities, and engage in baseless, reputation-ruining gossip?

Employees have choices to make. While adapting to one's corporate culture is generally recommended, emulating a leader's bad behavior is not. Instead, employees need to think about their own reputations and personal standards of conduct. They can become role models themselves by extending simple courtesies such as listening attentively and valuing others' opinions. They can challenge and report disrespect when they experience it or witness it. They can and must take responsibility for their actions. And if the culture becomes just too toxic, they can leave and find a respectful work environment. They do exist.

Duncan: *It's widely agreed that people don't leave jobs, they leave people. In light of this obvious truism, why do so many organizations tolerate disrespectful behaviors?*

Thomas: Presumably recognizing the harsh prospective consequences, it's difficult to imagine why an organization would tolerate disrespectful behavior. But some do. It might be because they are under pressure and feel there's no time for niceties. It could be because they view politeness as a weakness and want to be seen as aggressive and strong. They could be testing employees to see how they respond to incivility and whether they brush it off, defend themselves, retaliate, complain, or sulk. They might be trying to evaluate an employee's trustworthiness and loyalty or they could be encouraging rivalries. It could be a power play or they may just delight in disharmony. They might be unaware of the consequences of disrespect or they simply might not care.

Creating a safe, civil workplace takes deliberation and resolve on the part of management. Respect always starts at the top.

Duncan: *What are some specific practices you've seen that encourage (and reward) respectful behavior in the workplace?*

Thomas: It's not dissatisfaction with money, benefits, or workloads that cause people to leave organizations. Lack of appreciation is the reason 79% of employees give for quitting their jobs. Given the high costs of turnover and its effect on productivity, why showing appreciation is not at the top of every boss's list is inexplicable. Thanking someone in a company newsletter or at weekly or quarterly meeting costs nothing. Yet, it reaps exponential returns in terms of morale and goodwill.

Zappos, the online retailer, rewards good behavior with "Zollars" (Zappos dollars) and peer-to-peer "Wow" awards from coworkers. Anything from holding a door open, to smiling, offering help, volunteering, or tidying a common area might qualify someone for a $50 reward. Rewards are getting creative. Among the available options are professional development opportunities, charitable donations, travel subsidies, memberships, VIP parking, house-cleaning, meal deliveries, and the always popular time.

Simple is often better. A handwritten note of thanks from the company president is still the most sought-after and valued recognition of all. (See chapter 24, Close Encounters: Leadership and Handwritten Notes.)

Duncan: *Professional reputation—or personal brand—is vitally important. As Amazon CEO Jeff Bezos says, "Your brand is what people say about you when you're not in the room." In today's workplace, what are the three or four most important ingredients of a positive personal brand?*

Thomas: "Personal branding" is not new. One's reputation and all of the things that contribute to it have always mattered. The Internet is what makes the concept of personal branding so topical today.

Today we are all under a magnifying glass with our personal brands visible to the entire world. While all elements of a personal brand are significant, some are of even greater importance because other elements derive from them.

First up is attitude. It's estimated that attitude accounts for 85% of success. Treating everyone with respect and dignity, maintaining a can-do approach, and offering help, congratulations, thanks, and apologies are just some of the ways our positive attitudes come through.

Attire is also critically important. It conveys competence, judgment, and respect, or the lack thereof. Appropriate attire is always dictated by the culture of the organization that employs us. Whether in a buttoned-up suit, a uniform, or a hoodie, we dress to meet expectations, not to defy them.

Work ethic is certainly among the top three. Are we team players who meet deadlines or do we make excuses? Is the quality of our work exemplary or is it incomplete and error-ridden? Do we give credit when due, or keep it all to ourselves?

Paying attention to attitude, attire and work ethic practically guarantees a brand that reflects well upon the individual, vital in an increasingly competitive global workplace.

Duncan: *Ignoring relatively benign disrespect can send the unintended signal that increasingly boorish behavior might be tolerated. Without coming across as haughty or unapproachable, what can a person do to set boundaries on behavior that is acceptable to him or her?*

Thomas: Disrespectful behavior is rampant, but it's not always intended. Any combination of stress, fatigue, and fear can get the better of an otherwise amiable coworker. To make sure you don't personalize what is not meant personally, try to understand and empathize with the person. (This is a good strategy because you may need someone's understanding in the future.)

Next, consider the environment. If you recently joined a corporate culture where profane language and ribald humor are the norm with no particular harm intended, any attempt to change it may label you prudish or judgmental. Do not lecture or complain. Instead, avoid uncomfortable situations or ignore them as much as you can. Choose battles and approach them carefully. If someone makes a remark that sounds disrespectful there's a chance it was misheard or taken out context. Approach the person privately to clarify what was meant. Then share the impact of the words and ask if she could use different words in the future. If the behavior continues, let the person know your concentration and productivity are being affected, and your ability to work with her compromised. Communicate that you plan to seek a new team/position/location within the organization and to enlist the help of management to do so.

Being civil does not require that we accept legitimately unacceptable behavior, only that we confront it in a civil way.

Duncan: *Many people seem to be almost anatomically attached to their cell phones. What is some of the cell phone etiquette you recommend?*

Thomas: Statista.com estimates that by 2019, 67% of the world's population, or more than five billion people, will be mobile phone users. And it's not just millennials who are glued to their phones. People of all ages use their phones constantly, and in every setting imaginable. Weddings, funerals, churches, synagogues, doctors' offices, locker rooms—apparently no place is off limits. This non-stop usage takes a huge toll upon relationships, safety, and sleep.

To keep in touch and keep relationships intact, use good judgment. Even if the culture of a group condones it, don't be the first to use your phone because a domino effect will rapidly take hold. Generally, do not use a phone at a family, business, or social meal, in others' homes, or without permission. Certainly do not use a phone in serious or somber settings where someone's concentration or sensibilities may be affected. If you must use a phone while walking or driving, be keenly aware of pedestrians, objects, and traffic.

According to the Centers for Disease Control, each day nine people die from distracted driving and more than 1,000 are injured. Remember that the person physically in front of you takes precedence over any incoming or outgoing text or call. Yes, you may need to respond to an emergency message, but most communication is not worth the risk of damage to a relationship.

Duncan: *Social media have created a broad panorama of challenges and opportunities. What advice do you offer professional people regarding their digital footprints?*

Thomas: The current conversation about enhanced Internet privacy notwithstanding, we should understand that anything we share in cyberspace is viewable, or at least accessible, to anyone else—forever.

It remains to be seen whether, when, or how Internet service providers improve their protection of users' privacy. Even Google's new "Confidential mode," which prevents an email from being printed or forwarded, doesn't actually delete email. It merely revokes a recipient's access to it after a designated period of time.

Our "digital footprints" are growing bigger by the second. With every post, share, tag, snap, or like, we leave traces of digital DNA that cannot be expunged. And we jeopardize safety, reputations, and finances—ours and others'—in the process.

But we can take some control. Start by conducting an online audit and deleting any questionable posts. Ask friends to do the same. Share nothing that could possibly be deemed racist or sexist. Always use good taste—no photos of risqué clothing, offensive gestures, drunken revelry, or other less-than-discreet activities. Avoid venting anger, arguing, or over-sharing online. Treat others with respect, be accountable, and strive to post relevant, useful information that you would be comfortable with anyone seeing, future employers and grandmothers alike.

Personal application:

- What are some of your conscious behaviors that you intend to demonstrate respect for others?

- What are some things you can do to improve in your practice of appropriate etiquette?

- How can you best demonstrate appreciation for others in your workplace?

15

ROK (Return On Kindness): It's More Than Just Being Nice

Expert: Jill Lublin, business coach, author of *The Profit of Kindness*

What you'll learn: Kindness is not simply a nice-to-have social trait. It's an important ingredient in effective relationships, especially if you're a leader.

During 40 years of consulting and executive coaching, I've worked with hundreds of leaders. The ones who are world-class, who produce consistently great results, have some characteristics in common—smarts, a sense of vision, a deep understanding of their business, willingness to make tough decisions.

These are textbook qualities of great leadership. But one quality demonstrated by the best leaders I've known is seldom recognized: kindness.

Yes, kindness. Some people still seem to regard kindness as a nice-to-have-but-unnecessary personality trait. In fact, some prominent business people have been practically deified in their reputations for harsh and even barbarous treatment of others.

Finally, we have an opposing view. Business coach Jill Lublin has written *The Profit of Kindness: How to Influence Others, Establish Trust,* and *Build Lasting Business Relationships.* This is not a soft-and-cuddly treatise on good manners. It's a guide to using kindness currency to get great results, loaded with specific examples of how and why kindness really works.

Rodger Dean Duncan: *In a world of tough-minded executives, why do so many people still seem to reject the notion that it's easier to attract flies with honey than with vinegar?*

Jill Lublin: As Berny Dohrmann, founder of CEO Space International, puts it: "Competitive thought is the source of every problem in relationships." We've been indoctrinated that if we don't protect our turf, someone will invade it. Even the economy is based on competition. If you want to have more clients, sell more products or services, gain profits, you have to top any other business offering the same. Our end-goal inevitably becomes domination, monopoly.

But the same network, CEO Space International, shows us that success can also be achieved through compassion and connection. In this network are executives who might be in the same line of businesses. But instead of stabbing each other in the back, they share their struggles and, in return, hear "I have a solution for you and it will save you time and money." Through this collaboration, these people offer better customer experience that eventually leads them to profits.

Duncan: *How can a person practice kindness so it becomes an automatic, default behavior?*

Lublin: Kindness and good character go hand-in-hand. When you have good character, you possess the characteristics of kindness that let people know that you are caring, respectful, responsible, trustworthy, etc. Fred Kiel, founder of KRL International, published research that demonstrates how the moral principles of integrity, responsibility, forgiveness and compassion produce life-affirming inner change. Make a conscious effort to tap these four as you act or decide.

When communicating, ask yourself if you're displaying integrity. Are you telling straight facts or are you misleading? When you have made an error, ask yourself if you are being responsible. Are you going to own and correct the mistake or are you going to blame somebody else? Practice touching the core of your humanity and not reacting impulsively. As you make it a habit, you will notice inner change gradually. Soon enough, it will be second nature.

Duncan: *Attachment and engagement are essential to high performance in organizations. What role does kindness play?*

Lublin: Workforce engagement is the outcome organizations achieve when they connect employees both professionally and emotionally with the organization, the people in it, and the work they do. And what does kindness do? Kindness produces positive social connections. Kind organizations have kind leaders who drive the flow of positivity within the workplace.

Suzy Welch says leaders must serve as Chief Meaning Officers who show employees how their work connects with the company's mission, and what's in it for them. They keep people challenged, they give people their attention, they foster autonomy, and they set aside time for their team. With kindness around them, people feel appreciated and valued. They perform better and stay loyal.

In one Gallup study engagement dropped to 2% among teams with neglectful managers. On the other hand, Businessolver, an employee benefits company, found that 33% of employees would change to more emphatic employers for equal pay while 20% would switch for less.

Duncan: *Having "an attitude of gratitude" sounds like an empty cliché to some. But how does an atmosphere of gratitude inspire people to do better and be better?*

Lublin: Lindon Crow, President of Productive Learning, once reminded me of the "spheres of influence." We cannot influence without positivity. He says, "As a leader, the way in which I walk into the door has an ability of leaving a trail of carnage or a trail of inspiration and motivation." By living out his own values, he believes that he can foster his employees' mission of kindness, and, in turn, the employees will positively impact their clients. That will start a cycle of growth and the cycle of a currency of kindness. Gallup reported that 67% of employees are happier and more productive when managers focus on the positive aspects of their performance. It's also an example of upstream reciprocity—people with a high propensity toward gratitude are likely to act in a similar helpful way both to their benefactors and to others.

Duncan: *In today's highly competitive business environment, "compassion" doesn't seem to be a behavior at the top of many people's to-do lists. What are they missing?*

Lublin: A lot. For one, free advertising.

Are you familiar with the viral story of Panera Bread? Brandon Cook's grandmother wished for a clam chowder when she got hospitalized. Brandon called Panera Bread only to find out that they serve clam chowder only on Fridays. Still, Brandon talked to the Store Manager, Susanne Fortier, who not only prepared the soup but also gave a box of cookies for Brandon's grandma. That post garnered more than 500,000 "likes" and 22,000 comments. When genuine acts of compassion are seen, it's hard not to be shared.

This occurred back in 2012. Even today, it's being shared. People will come across this, they will search for Panera Bread and, perhaps, visit their store. Without any effort, Panera Bread will gain another customer. No money, no strategy, just pure kindness.

Personal application:

- In what specific ways can you demonstrate integrity, responsibility, forgiveness, and compassion?

- How can you focus on the positive results produced in your organization without ignoring things that need improvement?

- Think of a time someone showed genuine kindness to you. How did it make you feel about that person? How did it make you feel about yourself?

16

The High Cost of Compromise

Commentary: Rodger Dean Duncan

What you'll learn: Compromise can be seductive and subtle. And it can have life-or-death consequences.

In Washington nowadays at least some of the people are clamoring for compromise. You'll notice that it's always those in the minority who do the clamoring.

Compromise can be good in politics. In many other fields it can spell calamity.

One famous example is especially instructive.

A while back I visited with Harold W. Gehman. He prefers to be called Hal. Hal is a retired U.S. Navy admiral who served as a member of the Joint Chiefs of Staff, the Pentagon's top military decision makers. Hal was called on by President George W. Bush to head the special board investigating the *Columbia* Space Shuttle accident.

There is much to learn from the board's findings.

The investigation board set out to answer three questions. First, "What happened to the *Columbia*?" As anyone watching television on that Saturday morning can tell you, the *Columbia* disintegrated when it reentered the earth's atmosphere at 205,000 feet while traveling 14,000 miles per hour southwest of Dallas at about 8:00 a.m. Central time.

Although the *Columbia* scattered more than 84,000 pieces of debris across Texas and into western Louisiana, there were no witnesses to the accident. (Yes, millions of us saw the debris falling, but nobody saw the actual accident.)

The second question the board set out to answer: "Was whatever caused the accident an anomaly, or was it something that had occurred before without such consequences?"

If the answer to the second question was that the accident's cause had been seen before, then the third question had to be "Was the cause dealt with adequately?"

After thousands of man-hours of investigation, the board concluded that there were two causes to the *Columbia* accident. One was technical, the other was organizational.

The technical cause of the loss of the space shuttle *Columbia* occurred 16 days before the accident. It happened on launch. The shuttle was struck by a small piece of light-weight material similar to that of a Styrofoam cup.

The organizational cause of the accident was both complicated and simple. More on that later.

It's interesting to note that, prior to this launch of *Columbia*, there had been 113 shuttle flights. Most people are amazed by that number. It shows how routine space flight had become. As it turns out, "routine" is part of the danger.

Now, a bit of Shuttle 101.

When a shuttle lifts off the launch pad, it's bundled with three other huge pieces of apparatus. Two mammoth white rockets on the side of the shuttle are solid rocket boosters. They produce a total of five million pounds of thrust. After two minutes and 15 seconds, these two rockets are jettisoned and fall harmlessly into the ocean.

A big orange tank in the center of the bundle holds liquid fuel for the shuttle's three on-board engines. The tank is made of aluminum, and the fuel it holds is cold—roughly minus 450 degrees. Because something that cold produces dangerous ice in the humid Florida air at the launch site, the tank is covered with insulating foam. This foam was the technical cause of the *Columbia* accident.

Hal Gehman says the people in the space program had succumbed to "the Gamblers' Dilemma." On every single previous launch of a shuttle, the orbiter was damaged by foam striking it. And on every single previous launch the damage did not cause an accident. "The Gamblers' Dilemma" was the danger in forgetting that what happened in the past is in no way a guarantee of what may happen in the future (as the fine print in any financial prospectus reminds us).

Early in the shuttle program, falling foam was regarded as a "Level 1" hazard. The orbiter is covered with an extremely delicate thermal protection system that absolutely must remain intact. Upon reentering the earth's atmosphere, the orbiter is subjected to heat of up to 10,000 degrees Fahrenheit. Any compromise in the orbiter's outer skin can spell disaster.

But on 113 previous flights, damage from falling foam was within tolerable limits. So, over time, the engineers accepted the falling foam as a harmless, recurring reality. They even had a term for the phenomenon. They called it "a normalized deviance." Falling foam was "outside of specifications," but because it had not been a problem it was simply accepted.

A chilling part of this story is that "normalized deviance" also played a role in a previous disaster. Remember the Challenger tragedy in 1986? It was caused by leaking O-rings on the solid rocket booster. The O-rings had leaked on nearly every previous flight of the Challenger, but the "outside of spec" phenomenon had become accepted as tolerable.

This kind of compromise is the organizational cause of the *Columbia* accident. As Hal Gehman says, "Some engineers were yelling and screaming, 'We can't live with this,' while others were saying, 'No, no, it's okay. Don't worry about it.'"

In a world driven by schedules and budgets and political pressures, compromises are an inevitable part of the mix. Some of the compromises can be deadly.

Hal Gehman puts it into perspective: "The really scary thing about this history of anomalies is how cleverly they [the space program engineers and administrators] documented every time a piece of foam came off, which was on every flight. And it's scary how the recurring events were incrementally characterized as less and less serious. Somehow, man seems to think that by putting a different label on a bad thing he can diminish the danger of the bad thing."

What can we learn from all this?

There are so many easy, even logical, compromises available to us. Most of us know a correct principle when we see it. And many people have a finely-tuned ability to cut corners for the sake of convenience or some other arbitrary excuse. For evidence, just consider the lapses at Enron, Tyco, the *New York Times*, WorldCom, Wells Fargo and other organizations where corners were cut.

A helpful approach to the temptation of compromise is seen in the story of the father of teenagers. It may be only an urban legend, but it's instructive nonetheless.

The family had a high standard on what kind of movies were appropriate for viewing. The three teens in the family wanted to see a particular popular movie that—although was "mostly" okay—seemed to violate some of the family standards. The teens interviewed friends to get details on the movie. They compiled a list of pros and cons. They would use the list to persuade their dad that they should be allowed to see the movie despite its occasional lapses.

The father reviewed the list of "evidence" and promised to give them his answer in 24 hours.

The next evening he called his three teens into the kitchen. On the table he had placed a plate of brownies. He said he had carefully considered their request and had decided that if they would eat one brownie each he would let them see the movie. But just like the movie, he said, the brownies had pros and cons.

The pros were that they were made with the finest chocolate and other good ingredients. They were moist and fresh, made with an award-winning recipe.

The brownies had only one con. He had included a special ingredient—"just a little bit" of horse manure. But he had mixed the dough well. The manure probably couldn't even be tasted because the brownies were baked at 350 degrees and any bacteria from the manure had probably been destroyed. "Probably."

Therefore, if any of his children could stand to eat a brownie that included "just a little bit" of manure and not be affected by it, then he knew they probably would also be able to see the movie with "just a little bit" of smut and not be affected. "Probably."

The teenagers decided the movie wasn't that attractive after all.

The story is likely apocryphal, but it makes a good point. The next time we're tempted to compromise a principle, wouldn't it be great if a wise friend brought us back to reality by offering to whip up a batch of those special brownies?

Of course that's not the way it works. We make most decisions and choices on our own, without the coaching of others. And even if others *are* coaching us, they can be susceptible to the same compromises we are.

"Normalized deviance" is not unique to the space program. It can and does happen to anyone who toys with compromise.

Admiral Gehman certainly has it right. Putting an "acceptable" label on a dangerous thing is a perfect recipe for disaster.

Personal application:

- Where do you face the temptation to "cut corners" in your work? What, or whom, could that put at risk?

- What forms of "normalized deviance" can you see in your environment? What can you do to get things back on the proper course?

Trust and Teamwork

"If you want to go fast, go alone. If you want to go far, go together."

African Proverb

17

Want An A Team? It's All About Learning Curves

Expert: Whitney Johnson, coach and consultant, author of *Build an A Team: Play to Their Strengths and Lead Them Up the Learning Curve*

What you'll learn: Learning to practice "disruptive innovation" can be a huge advantage in managing your career.

Most leaders want to be liked and respected. They also want to inspire high performance. Fortunately, both are possible simultaneously.

But it doesn't happen without mindful attention to *engagement*. And engagement is all about learning curves.

Backed by more than 20 years of research, consulting and coaching, Whitney Johnson has plenty of hands-on experience working with teams. And her book *Build an A Team: Play to Their Strengths and Lead Them Up the Learning Curve* offers a step-by-step process for transforming a group of people into a high-powered and productive team.

Johnson shared some of her insights.

Rodger Dean Duncan: *An A Team, you say, is a collection of learning curves. What does that mean?*

Whitney Johnson: Picture an S. At the bottom of the S, the low-end, is inexperience. In the middle, the steep part, is engagement. At the high-end, the top of the S, is mastery. Every single person in your organization is on an S or learning curve. Every organization is a collection of these curves.

Based on our research, you optimize for innovation (that is, lower your "we're about to be disrupted score") as follows:

- 15% of your people at the low-end of the learning curve, where they are new to role, and therefore ask questions like "why do we do this the way we do it?" There's tremendous value to your organization that comes with inexperience.

- 70% of your team is in the sweet spot of their learning

curve. You typically get to this point after six months to a year in a new role or on a new project. You are feeling competent, and therefore confident. These are your most productive employees.

- 15% of your people are at the high-end of the curve. After two to three years in the sweet spot, people move into mastery. They know what they are doing. They are masters. They have a perspective, because they are atop the curve, that others don't. This is also a danger zone. Now that they're no longer learning, people can get bored. You want employees to at this point be for a year at most before you help them jump to a new learning curve.

Want to know if your company or organization is about to get disrupted? Take the pulse of your workforce. If too many people are at the high end, you are at risk.

Duncan: *You correctly say that change, not stasis, is the natural mode of human life … that change promotes growth while stasis results in decline. Then why do so many people seem to resist change?*

Johnson: We resist change for the same reason we resist jumping off of a cliff. Because it's scary. What we don't understand is that there really is no such thing as standing still. Meaning the top of the S we are on, that thing that looks like a plateau, is actually a precipice. It's the innovator's dilemma, but for people. Do I wait to get pushed or do I jump? Do I disrupt myself or get disrupted? My framework of personal disruption packs you that parachute, providing a structure to do this.

Duncan: *What is "disruptive innovation" and how can an organization help its people practice it in managing their own individual learning?*

Johnson: Just as a disruptive low-end product can like Pac-Man eat away at the market share of an incumbent (as Netflix did to Blockbuster), personal disruption is about the movement from the bottom of a learning curve (like when I started as a stock analyst) to the top, and then jumping to the bottom of the next. To learn, leap and repeat. This drives engagement. Engaged people innovate. Companies with engaged people get ahead of the competition. They don't get disrupted. They disrupt.

Duncan: *What common practices by managers are most likely to produce* *the unintended consequence of damaging engagement of workers?*

Johnson: Here are three of the most common mistakes:

1. Hire people for proficiency, not potential, at what should be the low-end of a learning curve. It will be masked initially because they are acclimating, but once they do, they'll be bored.

2. As they move up the learning curve into competence, and are looking like high-potentials, we become afraid that they will fail, and so we stop challenging them. In the sweet spot, people need more, not less challenge.

3. At the high end of a curve, when people have mastered their role, and are bored, instead of finding something new for them to do, we keep them right where they are.

Duncan: *During the first six months after bringing someone onto a team, what are the most critical things to do to help the new hire succeed both short- and long-term?*

Johnson: First, set short-term goals. Clearly define one or two projects for your new employee. Provide clear budgets and precise deadlines. This de facto constraint gives your new employee something to bump up against to assess how well they are doing. Like a skateboarder who gets quick and useful feedback about their various tricks (in the form of falling on asphalt), the new hire will know X leads to success; not doing X you'll crash and burn.

Second, build out their internal network. Provide a specific list of people to reach out to. Give them credit for doing this. Introduce them to people they need help from and people they can provide help to. The more people they know, the more potential influence they have, the better their ability to get something done.

Duncan: *What are the smartest questions to ask (and answer) in helping a team recover from a failure to meet a goal?*

Johnson: Here are some of my favorites:

1. Why did the failure happen?

2. What process was not in place that could be improved?

3. Was the failure a result of a lack of effort or due to trying something new and having it not work?

4. Is this person or team failing because they are in the wrong role?

5. Are unrealistic expectations (on my part) as a leader partly to blame for the failure?

6. Could expectations be managed differently?

7. How quickly will you recover from this failure?

8. What important lesson did you learn? In other words, now that you've invested in this mistake, what will your return be on this investment?

Personal application:

•   In what ways are learning curves working (or failing to work) in the development of the teams where you play a part?

•   What can be done to help ensure that people continue to learn in your organization?

•   What are you doing to ensure your own continuous learning?

18

When People Take Pot Shots at Your Good Idea

Expert: Samuel B. Bacharach, organizational behavior specialist, author of *The Agenda Mover, Get Them on Your Side* and other books

What you'll learn: The ability to advance a worthy agenda will set you apart from the crowd.

In this age of rapid-fire change, having a good idea is not enough. A lot of people have good ideas. Having charisma and gravitas is not enough. A lot of people are impressive.

One thing that sets real movers and shakers apart from the rest of the crowd is the ability to *produce.*

Effective leaders—those who know how to advance an agenda—prepare for the inevitable resistance. They know what it looks and sounds and smells like and they know how to deal with it.

That's the premise advanced in *The Agenda Mover: When Your Good Idea Is Not Enough,* a great book by Cornell University professor Samuel Bacharach.

Don't shy away from Sam's impressive academic credentials. He's no ivory tower theorist. He and his colleagues deliver leadership development training around the globe. A specialist in organizational behavior, Sam talks and teaches in the language of a man who understands the real world of real business.

Here are some no-nonsense ideas you can use.

Rodger Dean Duncan: *One of my early mentors told me that a leader's key role is to "get good stuff done." I suppose you would agree with that?*

Samuel Bacharach: Certainly. We spend a lot of time training leaders in organizations but we ignore the one critical reality, and that is, when trying to move change and innovation in organizations, you have to be an agenda mover. All the charisma, all the authenticity, all the brilliance, all the good ideas amount to nothing if you don't know how to move an agenda through organizational complexity, turf, and multiple businesses. You may be a brilliant engineer heading an R&D unit, you may be in charge of sales in the Midwest, seeing new possibilities. You may even be CEO. To make sure that organizations don't get stuck and ensure that they thrive and are constantly changing and innovating, we must train individuals at all levels of organizations in the core skills necessary to move agendas.

Duncan: *You say "anticipation" is a critical but unheralded leadership skill. What are some examples?*

Bacharach: We have this mundane notion that organizations are rational systems in which good ideas naturally emerge. The reality is that good ideas are simply not enough—and certainly not in a world of sprawling organizations with embedded interest groups, divergent agendas, and mixed priorities.

In trying to move change or an innovation, too many leaders are obsessed with the quality of their ideas. But as we all know, organizations are turf-ridden with multiple interests, and nothing is easy as simply saying, "I have a good idea." At all levels of the organization, leaders need the political skills to mobilize support for their innovation and their ideas. While innovation and ideation are remarkably popular, nothing gets done unless these are paired with the political ability to work ideas through the maze of the organization. The Agenda Mover is that person who can move his ideas.

Smart agenda movers know that once they have an idea, the first thing they must do is anticipate where others are coming from. Even the best ideas will go nowhere if you don't anticipate the potential resistance of others. Anticipating resistance can't be an afterthought. Leaders need to anticipate resistance early in the change or innovation process.

Duncan: *Can you give an illustration?*

Bacharach: One example of not anticipating where others are coming from is when Steve Jobs went up against John Sculley and the Apple board in 1985. Jobs failed to understand the magnitude of the resistance. He thought he could push the Macintosh because of the nature of his revolutionary ideas. By the time the resistance became obvious, there were repercussions. That said, Jobs learned his lesson and later in his career became a true agenda mover.

Duncan: *So it's really critical to understand the "mental maps" of people who resist your agenda.*

Bacharach: Absolutely. In any organizational setting there are four critical mindsets that leaders need to be familiar with in moving their agendas.

- First we have the Traditional mindset. Traditionalists have modest goals, push for incremental change, and put a constant emphasis on precedent. They are by far the most conservative force in the organization.

- Next we have the Adjuster mindset. Like the Traditionalists, Adjusters are conservative but are willing to entertain change when absolutely necessary. Their motto is, "We'll cross that bridge when we come to it."

- Then we have the Developer mindset. Developers are grounded visionaries committed to transformation but they are cautious, planning at every stage.

- Finally, there is the Revolutionary mindset. Revolutionaries seek the broadest and most immediate change.

These are the four pillar agendas, or mindsets, that lie at the heart of any change or innovation. The problem that leaders have in moving change is that they don't anticipate where others are coming from. And when they do, they don't delve deeply enough to understand their core agenda. That is, are the people they need on their side Traditionalists? Or are they Adjusters or Developers? Maybe they are Revolutionaries? Agenda movers understand on a basic level where others in their organization are coming from.

A classic mistake that leaders make in anticipating an agenda is that they reduce agenda style to personality. While someone may be a Traditionalist on one issue, they may be a Revolutionary when it comes to something else.

Savvy leaders—true agenda movers—deeply understand these mindsets and understand the positions that these archetypes are likely to take, allowing them to be prepared to argue for their position.

Duncan: *The "yes-but" game is a common form of resistance to change. As you know, that's when someone softens a challenge to your idea by saying something like "Yes, of course we need to adjust the production schedule, but your approach troubles me." What are the most common "yes-but" criticisms a leader should expect?*

Bacharach: One mistake that leaders make is not anticipating the agendas of others. A second mistake that leaders make is not anticipating the specific language of resistance. We often talk about leaders doing their "homework" before going to a meeting. One of the best ways of doing homework is focusing on the challenges you face when getting in front of a group of people. You may be an engineer in Bangalore trying to convince headquarters in California for some seed money to develop a prototype. You may be a division head wanting to spin into another market or business line. Now you have to get the support you need. Your next challenge is focusing on the language of resistance.

People often think there are multiple arguments that can be made to counter a given point. Whenever I get in front a group, they tell me there are hundreds of arguments. At the core, there seem to be about seven types of arguments that people make in an organizational setting.

I call these the "seven yes-but arguments." They are nuanced. They're not the classic "got-you game." Every one of the yes-but arguments feigns a degree of acceptance, but with a disproportionate amount of hesitation. The person who makes one of the arguments is not *against* innovation and change. It's just that they want some things "clarified." In a corporate setting, leaders need to be aware of the seven yes-but arguments, which include the following:

1. **Your Idea Is Too Risky.** For those who make this argument, the risk is never worth the potential pay-off.

2. **Your Idea Will Make Things Worse.** As bad as things are, these resistors will claim that whatever feeble attempts you make will only further deteriorate a bad situation.

3. **Your Idea Won't Change a Thing.** The critics who make this argument attempt to puncture the leader's confidence and make the leader's effort seem insignificant at best or not worth the effort at worst.

4. **You Don't Know the Issues Well Enough.** Detractors who say this undermine the leader's legitimacy, experience, and depth of knowledge.

5. **You're Doing It Wrong.** This is the easiest argument to make, as there are many paths from point A to point B.

6. **It's Been Done Before.** This is an argument that is almost always used for the organizational newcomer.

If it didn't work last week or last year, why should it work now?

7. **You Have Ulterior Motives.** In other words, you are only doing this because it will benefit you personally.

Duncan: *What are some effective ways for reacting to "yes-but" arguments?*

Bacharach: In responding to the yes-but arguments, it's important to weigh your reaction. The litmus test of your pragmatic leadership is how you react to criticism.

You might confront the other party and charge them with making false or inaccurate claims. You could try to delegitimize your challengers by showing the weaknesses of their position. You may avoid your challengers, and look for support elsewhere and minimize your engagement with them. Whichever route you choose, you must be able to absorb their blows, respond to their comments, and—if they make some good points—incorporate what they say into your strategy.

Agenda movers don't let a well-delivered barb deflate their confidence. They don't get involved in an escalating competition of egos. Agenda movers know that letting criticism get personal will blur their objectivity, absorb their time and energy, and make others think that their ego is more important than seeing their idea come to fruition. Agenda movers know that getting involved in a competition of egos can easily get them thrown out of the game.

Rodger Dean Duncan: *When a leader is working to mobilize support for an idea or course of action, what are some of the most effective persuasion strategies?*

Bacharach: Leaders try to get individuals and groups to commit to an agenda. They try to get groups and individuals to commit to a change effort, new technology, new policy, new innovation, etc.

To achieve this, there are three basic things that leaders have to deal with. First, they have to establish their credibility and the credibility of their ideas. Second, they have to justify the timing of these ideas. Third, they have to deal with the anxiety other people may have. These are the things that agenda movers do to get people to shift their priorities and get behind their efforts.

It's important to remember that your credibility depends on both the worthiness of your ideas and your trustworthiness. Sometimes it's difficult for others to separate you from your ideas. The support you receive for your idea depends on whether others view you has having the credibility to push your idea forward. If others perceive that you or your idea is not credible, it's unlikely that you can form, let alone sustain, a coalition of support.

Duncan: *Building a coalition requires more than just tossing an idea on the table.*

Bacharach: Yes. Leaders often put too much emphasis on their great ideas without going deeply enough into their own credibility. Do they have the expertise? Do they know what's going on? Can they deliver? That's what people want to know.

Once you've established credibility, you have to answer the question, why now? What's the urgency? Are the customers expecting it? Is there external pressure for other sources? Are your competitors doing it? Do the numbers tell you it's time to move? To get the support you need, you must justify why you're taking action.

Finally, you have to appreciate the anxiety that people may feel in getting behind your ideas. You have to deal with their notion of risk. What does it mean for them and their people if the idea fails? Are you as a leader willing to make sure that the fallout doesn't impact them?

Duncan: *It's not unusual for a leader to misread the levels of support for an idea. What do you regard as keys to evaluating support accurately?*

Bacharach: One of the things leaders should do is to see support as a holistic notion. One of the mistakes leaders make is thinking there are two choices: support or no support. Agenda movers know there are shades of support. Active support is when a person or group gets behind you completely, but this may be more than you want. Passive support is when they're in your corner but not necessarily heavily involved. Weak support is when they are almost invisible and don't get in your way. There is a time and place for getting different types of support, and you have to gauge the type of support you need.

In the early stages of a new idea, maybe all you can get is weak support. Be happy for that. It's better than no support. You may not want active support at this juncture. Active support means that you are enmeshed in the interests of others. Agenda movers need to gauge the type of support they want. The real issue is over- or under-estimating the type of support they need.

Duncan: *Concerns about turf encroachment are often part of resistance to* *change. How can a leader deal with such concerns?*

Bacharach: Broad change initiatives make it difficult for people to protect old turf and old ways of doing things. New ideas may imply an infringement on the status and power held before. An agenda mover must take these concerns seriously and think of ways to preserve the status and resources of key stakeholders while implementing the new agenda.

Engaging in turf protection makes sense. While it may be necessary to break down turf to move an agenda forward, it is also important to assure individuals that their support of your initiative will not necessarily come with the loss of power, prestige, or control—in short, turf. What you need to do is to find a way to recognize and value every party involved, without giving them the sense that something is being taken away from them.

Note: For more great ideas on how to lead change, see Sam's latest book *Transforming the Clunky Organization: Pragmatic Leadership Skills for Breaking Inertia.*

Also see *CHANGE-friendly LEADERSHIP: How to Transform Good Intentions into Great Performance.*

Personal application:

- How can you best analyze your own agenda before moving ahead with implementation?

- Which of the mindsets listed do you think best describes your own? How can this self-awareness be helpful to you?

- Before you even propose an idea, how can you prepare for the "yes-but" arguments? How can that preparation not only help you with implementation, but improve the idea itself?

19

Earning and Keeping Trust: It's a Learnable Skill

Expert: Stephen M.R. Covey, leadership and culture authority, author of *The Speed of Trust: The One Things That Changes Everything*

What you'll learn: Genuine trust is an indispensable part of any healthy relationship or brand reputation. And there are specific behaviors to help earn and keep it.

Trust is the operating system of every relationship.

Think about that metaphor: *operating system.* You can have great software programs installed on your computer. But if the computer's operating system has a glitch, nothing seems to work right.

In your work environment you can have world-class processes in place, backed up by well-conceived procedures. But if trust is fragile, you can never achieve consistently good results.

In personal relationships, trust is always the key. It's possible to like and even love someone. But if strong trust is not part of the relationship it can never reach its full potential.

Honesty, of course, is a component of trust. Yet some people can be basically honest but simply unreliable. Reliability is also a matter of trust.

Nobody understands trust issues better than Stephen M.R. Covey, author of the bestselling book *The Speed of Trust.* I've known Stephen for many years, and sat down with him to explore the role of trust and trust-building in every facet of our lives.

Rodger Dean Duncan: *In your work with individuals and organizations, you talk about "low-trust taxes" and "high-trust dividends." What are some examples?*

Stephen M.R. Covey: Trust always affects two measurable outcomes: speed and cost. When trust goes down—in a relationship, on a team, in a company, in an industry, with a customer—speed decreases with it. Everything takes longer. Simultaneously, cost increase. Redundancy processes, with everyone checking up on everyone else, cost more. In relationships, on teams, in companies, that's a tax. I call it a low-trust tax where literally everything is being taxed off the top. Where trust is low, everything takes longer and costs more.

The opposite is true as well. When trust goes up in a relationship, or on a team, in a company, in an industry, with a client, with a customer—speed goes up with it and cost comes down. Everything happens faster and everything costs less because trust has been established. That's a high-trust dividend. It's really that simple, that real, that predictable.

Duncan: *What are some illustrations?*

Covey: After the 9/11 terrorist attacks, our trust and confidence in flying went down. So we took steps to prop it up. We increased security and beefed up all the procedures associated with flying. Those steps were helpful, but they came at a price. Traveling by air now takes longer and costs more. I'm grateful for the security. It's important. But it came at a price. We had to prop up the lack of trust. It took time, cost money.

With corporate scandals—Enron, Worldcom, and the like—our trust in public markets went down because we realized there are some people out there "cooking the books." Trust went down. Congress stepped in and passed Sarbanes-Oxley [Accounting Reform Act]. Sarbanes-Oxley is not trust itself. It's a series of rules, regulations and compliance measure intended to help deal with fragile trust. It's helped in that the markets didn't collapse, as they perhaps could have. But it came at a price. Sarbanes-Oxley takes a whole lot of time and costs a whole lot of money to implement. Speed goes down, cost goes up.

That's the consequence of low trust. You see it in any relationship, in any business. When trust erodes, speed drops and cost rises.

Duncan: *What about the opposite effect?*

Covey: Warren Buffet, considered by many to be the most business-savvy investor around, is able to do huge business deals quickly because there's high trust, because he's so credible. He extends trust, he builds it fast, and he operates on that premise. He often closes major business deals in less than a month, with little diligence. It would probably be foolish for most of us to try to do such a deal. But in his case, his credibility is so high, the trust is so high, he's able to do things probably the rest of us couldn't.

Duncan: *That's a good anecdotal example. What hard data do you have on high-trust dividends?*

Covey: A Watson Wyatt study shows that high-trust organizations outperform low-trust organizations by 286% in total return to shareholders. That's stock price plus dividends—three times higher.

Look at the 100 best companies to work for in America. To be on that list of the Great Places to Work, you must have high trust. Trust is actually 60% of the criteria. You won't be on the list if the trust is not high, even if you have a lot of other great things about your company. The companies on that list outperform the market by 288%. So you've got a nearly three times multiplier when trust is operating as a dividend in your organization.

We see the impact of trust in outsourcing relationships. A Warwick Business School study in the UK showed that outsourcing relationships based on trust, as opposed to those based upon the service agreements—the contract only—the trust relationships outperform the others by 40%. They call it the 40% dividend.

You see the impact of trust in schools. High-trust schools have a 3.5 times greater probability of improving test scores than do low-trust schools.

It goes on and on and on. You see high trust is a dividend, just as surely as low trust is a tax. And suddenly the soft topic becomes hard-edged, it becomes economic.

Duncan: *If trust is a competency as well as a character trait, what are some of the specific behaviors that can be taught to people and emphasized in an organization's performance culture?*

Covey: When people look at trust through this fresh lens, they typically "get it" right away. Then they want the framework for building and maintaining trust. So we teach about integrity and intent, the dimensions of credibility that are vital to establishing trust with people. But it's insufficient by itself to say, okay, I'm credible. At that point it becomes all about our behavior, the way we interact, how we do it.

We've identified the 13 behaviors that are common to high-trust people, high-trust leaders, high-trust teams, high-trust companies. They consistently behave in these ways, and they avoid the opposite behaviors, or the counterfeits.

One of the behaviors is to *create transparency*. Creating transparency means I'm trying to be as open, as authentic, as real as possible. Transparency means "see-through." The opposite of this behavior is to be obscure, to be covered, hidden. The counterfeit is when people operate with hidden agendas. They tell you "Here's what I'm trying to do." But they have another agenda that they're not disclosing. People sense that, and it makes trust fragile. They withhold. But creating transparency wherever possible will accelerate the building of trust.

Another high-trust behavior is to *talk straight*. You are candid, real, open and honest with people. The opposite of that is lying. Of course lying obviously depletes trust. Lying generally doesn't work. The danger here again is the counterfeits. The counterfeit behavior to talking straight is that people spin, they position, they posture. They technically tell the truth, but not all of it. They leave the wrong impression. The net effect is that we aren't quite sure we can trust them. Many politicians are so filled with spin that people aren't quite sure if they can trust what they hear. And they generally don't because they feel like it's just spin, as opposed to real, authentic, straight talk. And on and on and on. There are 13 of these behaviors.

Duncan: *What are some others?*

Covey: Another one is keeping commitments. The fastest way to build trust is to make a commitment and keep it, then repeat that process. The opposite is when you violate a commitment. The counterfeit is where you overpromise and under-deliver, so you're "sort of" delivering on what you said but not as much.

And so it is—practicing accountability, clarifying expectations, showing loyalty, demonstrating respect. I'm just naming some of these behaviors. The point is that rather than remaining this elusive, intangible, mystical concept, trust can be quantified. We can show the credibility and behaviors that enable trust to be built and built fast, in a relationship, on a team, and in an organization. That's exciting, because then you can turn this into a strength and even a competitive advantage.

Many companies have significant trust problems that impose costly, hidden taxes. That's because people are behaving in counterfeit ways. They haven't learned the codified behaviors that will actually build trust. You can repair trust problem if they exist. Conversely, if trust is already good, you can build on that strength and double, triple, quadruple the dividend.

Duncan: *Trust obviously has a time component. But in some instances people don't have the luxury of a lot of time. For example, the nuclear power industry has an aging workforce. A lot of the really smart people are retiring in a short time period and the bench strength isn't what the industry would like it to be. The younger smart people coming into the industry don't have the luxury of 25 or 30 years to build up credibility. They need to have an impact virtually immediately. The margin of error doesn't allow for anything less. So how can the 13 behaviors accelerate the building of trust?*

Covey: The kind of environment you just described puts a greater premium on being good at building trust and doing it faster. That's why I call this The Speed of Trust. Once you've established trust, nothing is as fast as the speed of trust. You can move with incredible speed, like Warren Buffet does and like other leaders who have built huge trust accounts with their stakeholders.

The second part of the speed of trust is that once you understand what trust is—the components behind it, the dimensions around it, and especially the behaviors that build it—you can establish trust far faster than you might think possible. It doesn't have to be something that takes you forever. Yes, sometimes restoring violated trust will take time, and you can't force a process. But you can accelerate it. And you can accelerate it greatly by understanding and applying and actually turning these behaviors into habits. As you do that, you build trust and you build it fast.

Duncan: *What's the key to accelerating the building of trust?*

Covey: Make it explicit. Right up front, make it a clear objective that you want to build relationships of trust, you want to build a team of trust, you want to build a culture of trust. It becomes almost your operating system, so to speak. The cultural operating system of your enterprise is to build a culture of trust. When that becomes explicit and deliberate, great things begin to happen. It raises the ante. People will hold you more accountable and will expect you to hold them more accountable.

Being explicit also accelerates the development of trust because people are aware that you're trying to do it—it's important to you. Then when you signal to people your behavior, you tell them what to look for. You tell them what you're going to be doing, things like this: "Look, it's important that we create a relationship of trust because with that we can move at greater speed and lower cost. It's a better quality of life. So here's what you can know about me. If I make you a commitment, you can know that I'm going to keep it." See, what you've done? You've signaled your behavior. You've told them what to look for. You're held more accountable now.

If you don't deliver on what you just said, then there's risk to that. You can lose trust faster. But when you do deliver, you can accelerate the building of trust. Because you've told them what to look for, they see it more clearly, more obviously, and they give you credit for it. And you literally accelerate the building of trust by behaving in these ways and by signaling to people your behavior. You've taken this concept and turned it into a skill, something that you can get good at, not as a form of manipulation because that would never work, but as a competence that is part of how you can lead and part of who you are. You're creating a culture of trust. That becomes an enormous performance multiplier for any leader, for any company.

Duncan: *Some people can be very good, very smart about learning behaviors, even exhibiting certain behaviors. Is it possible to fake it? What if a smart guy goes through a workshop and says to himself, "Okay, if that's what it's going to take for people to trust, I'll just pretend with these behaviors." How does that work?*

Covey: Well, it doesn't work. Someone might get away with it for a very short time, but they won't sustain it. Trust behaviors are not something you can fake. Maybe in the short run a manipulator can get away with it. But here's why it won't work in the long run. If you separate these behaviors from their foundation, which is credibility—that's your integrity, your intent or motive, your capabilities and your results—if you sever those, in the long run it won't work, it won't be sustainable. It will actually have the opposite effect. It will end up diminishing trust because people will become cynical. They will read through it, maybe not immediately, but they will ultimately. They'll sense what your real motive is, they'll see that what you're really doing is trying to adopt these behaviors as a form of manipulation, as a technique that's not tied to your character, competence, integrity, and intent. So the net effect will actually be a diminishing of trust.

Genuine trust is an inside-out process that begins first with your own credibility. You always start with self, your character, your competence. Then on that foundation of self-trust and credibility the behaviors can come to life. They work well, and they work fast. You will build trust very fast as you practice these behaviors. We've codified these and put them into a user-friendly training framework. When people see them, it's self-evident. And yet the common practice in most organizations remains the counterfeit behaviors, because that's what cultures typically tolerate or even encourage.

Personal application:

- What are some low-trust taxes that you might be inadvertently imposing on people?

- How could you use transparency, straight talk, and keeping commitments to increase or reinforce the trust people have in you?

- How can you be more explicit about your trust-building behaviors?

20

Boost Your Trust Quotient, Strengthen Your Relationships

Expert: Michelle Reina, coach and consultant, co-author of *Trust and Betrayal in the Workplace*

What you'll learn: It's possible to erode trust without even knowing it. Maintaining a positive balance in your "trust account" is critical to all your relationships.

On the political campaign trail, "trust" is a common theme in assessing both the attractiveness and electability of candidates. While most of us will never have our own trustworthiness measured by the pollsters, it's nevertheless a key ingredient of the personal "brand" we project in the marketplace of relationships.

Dr. Dennis Reina and Dr. Michelle Reina are experts on the subject. Their book *Trust and Betrayal in the Workplace* is excellent reading for anyone who's really serious about building effective relationships.

To sample their approach, I interviewed Michelle Reina.

Rodger Dean Duncan: *It's been said that a thousand tiny paper cuts can do as much damage as one deep stab wound. In the workplace, what are some of the seemingly harmless "trust paper cuts" that add up to produce feelings of betrayal?*

Michelle Reina: Business is conducted via relationships. Relationships that produce results are based on a foundation of trust. Every day, "trust paper cuts" are inflicted when people:

- Gossip, and backbite: Talk *about* each other rather than *with* each other when issues arise.
- Exclude others from decisions that impact their work.
- Withhold information or fail to act on requests for information promptly.
- Take more credit than is truly deserved.
- Change plans without consulting stakeholders.
- Fail to keep agreements, meet deadlines, or accept responsibility.
- Micromanage others' skills and abilities.
- Spin the truth rather than tell it like it is.

- Are late for work repeatedly.
- Blame others.
- Criticize to intimidate rather than improve other's behavior.

The most challenging aspect of "trust paper cuts"? About 90% of the time, people aren't even aware these behaviors are eroding trust. While the behaviors don't get addressed, they do *not* go unnoticed.

Duncan: *When people already trust us, what are some of the routine behaviors that reinforce and even strengthen that trust?*

Reina: Even in the most trusting relationships, people still let each other down. Disappointments, misunderstandings, and broken trust are natural outcomes of human relationships. The difference in high-trust relationships is that when trust is compromised, people work through the situation together. Instead of blaming or avoiding, they ask questions to understand the circumstances and check out assumptions. They revisit expectations, making the implicit explicit. They talk to each other with positive intent to learn, grow, and deepen their connection. Through this process, broken trust becomes a stepping-stone to stronger trust.

Duncan: *In some organizations, trust is embraced at the slogan level while inter-department competition is the norm. What's your advice in that kind of situation?*

Reina: We recommend leaders conduct an assessment to pinpoint systemic behaviors driving counter productive competition. They will discover self-serving behavior: people jockeying for position, hoarding information, not being responsive to others' needs or requests, and working at cross-purposes. Behind these behaviors, they will likely uncover internal competition for resources that is institutionally structured and rewarded. Or, a cultural ingrained attachment to *"This is the way it is and always has been."* Or, disincentives that impede inter-departmental collaboration.

Systemic competition breaks down collaboration, prevents people from doing their best work, and compromises trust. Only when identified and understood can behaviors driving unhealthy competition be redirected and positioned for trustworthy behavior to be the new collective goal.

Duncan: *The old proverb says the road to hell is paved with good intentions. What's the key to translating good trust intentions into observable, authentic behavior?*

Reina: First, do an internal check. Ask yourself what your intentions are. For instance, do you intend to listen openly to others' points of view? Do you intend to express interest in their work and discover what you can do to support their efforts? Do you intend to ask for feedback so that you can learn and grow? Getting clear on intentions is the first step to acting on them authentically.

Next, commit to behaviors that reflect those intentions. Often, behaving authentically requires humility, vulnerability, and compassion. Telling the truth about your thoughts and feelings can be uncomfortable. Being honest about what you can actually deliver and the skills you *don't have* takes courage. Yet, your transparency opens the door to deeper, more trustworthy relationships.

Duncan: *What's a workable formula for dealing with a betrayal of trust?*

Reina: There are seven steps.

- *Step One:* Observe and acknowledge what has happened. Recognize the impact of broken trust on your work and life.

- *Step Two:* Allow feelings to surface. Own the feelings associated with the breach of your trust. Are you confused, angry, hurt, shocked, or stunned?

- *Step Three:* Get support. Seek *objective* counsel to gain greater perspective.

- *Step Four:* Reframe the experience. Get curious. Consider the bigger picture, opportunities that may now be open to you, options you can consider. Reflect upon what the experience may teach you—about you, relationships and life.

- *Step Five:* Take responsibility. Take responsibility for restoring trust, even if you're not "at fault." Dig deep and learn the behaviors to practice that can keep the situation from happening again.

- *Step Six:* Forgive yourself and others. Release yourself from the weight of bitterness and resentment and empower yourself to approach others with compassion and understanding.

- *Step Seven:* Let go and move on. Disengage yourself from the grip of broken trust and move forward.

Duncan: *Most people know that behaviors either build or erode trust. What role does explicit conversation about behavior play in creating and maintaining trust?*

Reina: When people are honest and explicit they can raise each other's awareness of how their behavior is building or breaking trust. This raised awareness provides a reference point for feedback and open dialogue. A safe container is created to surface and work through breaches of trust and related issues and concerns.

Duncan: *Many people make commitments with good intentions, but then allow "new" issues to compete for their time and other resources. What are some tips for dealing with this "crescendo effect" so commitments and trust are not violated?*

Reina: Be honest—both with yourself and with others. Genuinely assess what you can and cannot do. Give yourself permission to say "no" or "not right now." Keep people informed of your current and intervening variables. If you do find your back up against a well, come clean immediately. Name the situation for what it is, and renegotiate. Everyone knows what it feels like to drop the ball. If you own your overextension right away, you'll often experience more compassion than you anticipated. You'll preserve and strengthen trust in your relationships.

Duncan: *During his long odyssey of perfecting the light bulb, Thomas Edison famously said "I have not failed. I've just found 10,000 ways that won't work." To inspire innovation, how important is it to foster an environment where "mistakes" are not punished?*

Reina: For innovation to flourish, mistakes need to be treated as opportunities to learn and grow, not faults to be punished. Courage and compassion are partners to innovation. When people make mistakes, what they need at their core is reassurance, and then insight to learn and grow from those mistakes. When judged and criticized, people contract, withdraw, and play it safe. The status quo becomes the new norm. Innovation ceases. We worked with a company that experienced a $2 million product recall because people didn't feel safe to admit mistakes. Creating an environment where mistakes are not punished is *that* important.

Duncan: *Some people who have been betrayed in the past find it difficult to extend trust to people who had nothing to do with the previous violation. What advice can you offer them?*

Reina: Notice your reluctance to trust. Pay attention to your tendency to generalize, judge, criticize, blame, or overlay something on another person that doesn't belong to them. Be willing to give this person a fresh opportunity and the benefit of the doubt. Remind yourself that they are *not* the ones who broke your trust in the past. Consider what it is you need to know, evidence you need to see, and perspective you need to gain and understand in order to feel safe to extend trust. Do you need specific information? Are there expectations you need clarified? Are there agreements that need to be met?

Rather than setting up the other person to have to wait for you to extend trust, ask for what you need. Give yourself permission to recover from the impact of previous betrayals so they do not impede your present relationships. Do your inner work so you can foster the healthy, trustworthy, productive relationships you want and need.

Personal application:

- What are some honest questions you could ask yourself to assess your behaviors that may build or erode trust?

- When someone else makes a mistake that affects you, what can they do or say to earn back or maintain your trust? How do you handle your own mistakes?

- How do you feel when someone is explicit about extending trust to you? Do you work doubly hard to prove that their trust is warranted? What does that tell you about how you could/should extend trust to others?

Culture

"Culture eats strategy for breakfast, operational excellence for lunch, and everything else for dinner."

21

Build Your Culture
By Design, Not By Accident

Expert: Ann Rhoades, coach and consultant, former Chief People Officer at Southwest Airlines, author of *Built on Values*

What you'll learn: Compromise professed values at your own peril.

Ann Rhoades is president of People Ink, which helps companies build values-based corporate cultures using the Values Blueprint principles. She was one of the five founding executives of JetBlue Airways and served as Chief People Officer at Southwest Airlines. In her book *Built on Values*, Ann shares in-depth details on hiring and keeping A Players. Ann's clients range from hospitals, banks and airlines to hotel chains, technology companies, and non-profit organizations.

Rodger Dean Duncan: *Your book* Built on Values *is about creating and maintaining a workplace environment that brings out the best in people. What have you found to be some of the most common misuses of the idea of values?*

Ann Rhoades: Giving only lip service to the values is a common mistake made by leaders. They plaster value statements or words on a wall or brochure but then fail to hold people accountable for the behaviors related to the values. Living a values model is all about behaviors and making the tough decisions around those values. I refer to it as getting the right results the right way! Not just advertising the right values, but putting the related behaviors into action and holding everyone accountable for those behaviors! No exceptions.

A cardiac surgeon in a prominent hospital system we worked with was so well known that the CEO was reluctant to let him go. But he eventually did because the surgeon's behaviors were the opposite of what the system held others accountable for. The hospital system found that it was one of their best decisions. That decision totally reinforced the principle that everyone would be held accountable, regardless of position or skill level.

Duncan: *You served as Chief People Officer at Southwest Airlines, a company known for its people-friendly culture and its consistently strong financial performance. What's the relationship between the two?*

Rhoades: It has been a long held premise of mine that leaders drive values and related behaviors. This creates the culture and ultimately determines performance. Southwest is a great example of a company that has lived this values model for more than 50 years and has continued to financially outperform their airline industry competitors.

Duncan: *Some organizations hire (or promote) leaders who have strong technical skills but who don't really measure up on the "people stuff." What advice do you offer on how to avoid this compromise?*

Rhoades: No exceptions on hiring people with the right values! At the start of JetBlue, we were required to hire maintenance players and we erred on hiring one particular person with outstanding technical skills but who did not lead or live the values model we had defined as part of our DNA. We soon realized our error and let this individual go. Once we put in a full behavioral hiring model around the values and related behaviors we were able to avoid for the most part these errors on an ongoing basis.

Duncan: *"Culture change" is on the minds of a lot of business people. What are the most critical steps for transitioning from one culture to another?*

Rhoades: The first step is gaining, through assessment, accurate data on what the "culture" really is versus what you want it to be. Gather feedback from both employees and customers. Then set about developing a change model that incorporates the values and behaviors you want to see throughout the organization. Build a hiring model around the respective behaviors, start communicating the new model for behavior, and set a time to start holding *everyone* accountable for these behaviors.

Also, build a reward and recognition program around these behaviors and start circulating stories about people living those values. Examples are critical and very impactful. It will take two to three years in a large organization and up to a year in most small companies to see the real results with both your employees and customers.

By the way, at some point the impact should be very noticeable to your customers. The comment and change should be obvious from the top and all around the organization. Treat this emphasis on values like any other well-organized project, with a Values Committee focusing on employees from all levels of the organization.

Duncan: *What are some of the keys to sustaining a values-centric organizational culture once it's established?*

Rhoades: The most important key is commitment at the top for the resources and time. Secondly, the values must be *lived*, and everyone needs to know this is not just some "Flavor of the Month" project. Values must become part of the DNA of the entire organization. That's when you will know your culture is working to the organization's advantage.

Duncan: *You talk a lot about finding, hiring, and keeping A Players. Tell us more about that.*

Rhoades: A Players are the people who genuinely live your company's values, every day. They're not always the high-flying world-beaters, and they don't even have to be part of your leadership team. They could be the front-line employees who smile, who go out of their way to be helpful, who care that things are done right. They are the people who help great companies and great leaders reach their full potential.

The most important positions in your organization are any that directly touch your customers. To your customers, your company is your front-line employees. If you want to attract and retain more customers, you must concentrate on putting A Players there first. Your organization will work as a well-oiled, value-generating machine only if you try, over time, to recruit, hire, train and reward as many A Players as you can.

Bottom line? The most successful companies are those that only hire A Players. They don't just hire the best of the available applicants simply because they need to fill a position. If they have to, they delay hiring until they find the A Players – those employees who do more than is required, live the company's values, and truly add value to the organization.

Of course, waiting to hire may mean that you have to delay the opening of a new facility, pay overtime, or be understaffed until you find the right people. A Players aren't always packaged the way you expect. But when you find them, they help you outperform the competition.

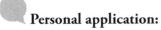

Personal application:

- Can you identify any disconnect between the values professed in your organization and the actual behaviors you observe? If so, what can you do to make the values more of a reality than a mere slogan?

- Regardless of your role, what can you do when you see someone behaving in ways that are contrary to the organizations professed values?

- Whom do you regard are your customers? What can you do to serve them in ways that reflect the values you treasure?

22

Culture, Leadership, and Performance

Expert: Edgar H. Schein, former MIT professor, noted author, widely regarded as the leading expert on organizational culture.

What you'll learn: "Culture" is all the relentless reinforcement of values and behaviors. It's not something you can "install" or "implement."

If there were an aristocracy among experts in the field of organizational development, Dr. Edgar Schein would likely be king.

For many years, he was a professor at the MIT Sloan School of Management. But he is known primarily for his prolific writing. He's author of more than a dozen books dealing with organizational performance issues. He holds degrees from the University of Chicago, Stanford, and Harvard. He's actually credited with "inventing" the term organizational culture.

I had the pleasure of serving with Ed on an industry advisory board. In addition to enjoying his magnificent intellect and wide-ranging interests, I find him to be wonderfully comfortable in conversation.

Rodger Dean Duncan: *Many years ago you were credited with coining the term "organizational culture." How do you find that term used and abused in the workplace today?*

Edgar Schein: Managers today understand the importance of culture as a factor in whether a company performs well or not. But many of them mistakenly believe they can arbitrarily decide whether or not you will have a good culture. They still don't understand that culture is a product of years of learning and experience, not something you "implement."

You can find companies whose culture helps them perform, but they acquired that culture over a period of years through leadership that worked. You can find in those same companies a drop in performance as the very culture that made the company successful became a liability when changes occurred in technology and in the market. This is the story of Digital Equipment Corporation. The same culture explained both its success and its failure.

Duncan: *In what important ways are culture and leadership fundamentally intertwined?*

Schein: In a mature company run by promoted general managers, as opposed to entrepreneurs or founders, the culture will reflect the past history of founders and leaders and will limit what kind of leadership is possible. If a new leader such as Carly Fiorina comes into a company (like she did at Hewlett-Packard with its long history and strong culture), there will be conflict between what the new leader tries to impose and what the culture will allow. The leader will win in such conflict only by firing large numbers of the carriers of the old culture, as turnaround managers usually do. The new leader can then start fresh by imposing new values and behavior patterns. But this is not a new culture until it succeeds for a number of years and becomes internalized by the employees.

So you can talk about *destroying* an old culture, but you cannot *create* or *impose* a new culture, only new values and behavior patterns.

When Lou Gerstner went into IBM, his success was based on figuring out what the culture was that had led to IBM's success. He noticing that the company had drifted away from some of the elements of that culture and he found a way to revive it. He worked on the culture by reviving and reinvigorating the best elements of what was there, not by "changing" the culture.

Duncan: *How does culture influence the leadership styles that "work" or fail to "work" in an organization?*

Schein: In general, the culture is stronger than the new leader and either limits or ignores new leaders who do not fit into the culture. The HP culture emphasized good relations between people, teamwork and humility. Carly Fiorina was able to impose some new goals and values, but her flamboyant style did not fit the culture at all and caused her ultimately to lose credibility and effectiveness. When John Sculley became CEO of Apple, he got the board to fire Steve Jobs. Then Sculley then was himself succeeded by several outsiders. The Apple culture never adapted to these new CEOs and limited their effectiveness because Apple was a technically based culture in which marketing-oriented CEOs never gained respect. When Steve Jobs came back, there was once again mutual congruence between the culture and the CEO's style and values.

Duncan: *We know that culture influences leadership. In what ways can* *leadership influence culture? For example, how can a leader reinforce the "helpful" aspects of a culture and dilute the culture's "harmful" attributes?*

Schein: In both cases, what the leader can do is to impose new behaviors and hope that performance improves. But the new behavior has to solve a problem. In a company whose culture leads salesmen from different units to visit the same customers and cause confusion and subsequent loss of those customers, the new leader might announce "from now on we will have a culture of teamwork in our sales force and we will work together."

But this will be meaningless until it is analyzed in *behavioral* terms. In this future "culture," what exactly are salesmen supposed to do differently? When the leader announces that from now on customers will be serviced by account teams of salesmen from different units and that individual salesmen will be rewarded by how the *account* does, and changes the structure and reward system to make that happen, then the new teamwork values will mean nothing. If that is implemented and succeeds over a period of time, then we can talk about a new "team culture."

Most culture change programs fail because they are just announcements of new values without a change in what new behavior will be required and how the structure and reward system will make that happen.

Duncan: *What are some of the early warning signs that an organization's culture needs to change?*

Schein: The warning signs are never "cultural." They are always performance issues that lead to specifying new behaviors needed to fix the problem. The culture gets involved if the new behavior won't work because of the culture. At Digital, they needed engineers to build simpler turnkey products to survive. But the engineering culture had been built on creating sophisticated, fun products, so the engineers did not respond to the new requirements.

To fix such a problem, you have to destroy elements of the old culture. But the focus has to remain on fixing the business problem and only then seeing how culture will aid or hinder the fix.

Duncan: *Various forms of resistance often thwart attempts at culture change. Why do people resist change, and what are the keys to turning resistance into support?*

Schein: Resistance to change is a normal response because what we are doing is based on past success, so why should we change what has worked in the past? The only way you can convince me to change is to show me that the old behavior no longer produces results and show me what new behavior would work better. You have to convince me that there is a business problem and show me how the new behavior that you are demanding will fix the problem and then provide me with the resources, and training in the new behavior and give me new incentives to learn it.

Personal application:

- In terms of observable behaviors, how would you describe the culture in your workplace?

- If you could wave a magic wand and change your workplace culture, what would that "new" culture look like?

- Since you *can't* wave a magic wand, what specific behaviors can you personally model (and encourage in others) that could produce a better culture?

23

How to Breathe Excitement into Mind-Numbing Work

Expert: Dan Cable, social psychologist, author of *Alive at Work: The Neuroscience of Helping Your People Love What They Do*

What you'll learn: Many people who are not engaged at work suffer from "learned helplessness." There are reliable cures.

Many organizations have it all wrong. They don't just need to motivate their people. They need to stop demotivating them.

If you've seen the results of recent research you know the typical workplace needs a major overhaul. In fact, multiple studies show that the modern workplace is plagued with chronically low levels of employee engagement. The Gallup organization estimates that disengagement is costing American companies $450 billion to $550 billion per year.

You might think such findings—which have remained painfully steady for many years—would result in changes. Yet many work environments still leave employees feeling stifled, unappreciated, and eager to update their LinkedIn profiles to search for the next job.

Social psychologist Dan Cable has some compelling ideas for making all this better. He's author of *Alive at Work: The Neuroscience of Helping Your People Love What They Do.*

In this conversation, Cable—a professor of organizational behavior at London Business School—offers suggestions on how to encourage self-expression and experimentation to help employees see how their work impacts and benefits others. In other words, how to replace discouragement with engagement.

Rodger Dean Duncan: *What are the most common demotivators in the workplace?*

Dan Cable: There are so many opportunities to demotivate someone, such as a colleague who is a "taker-jerk" and gets all the credit, or a power-hungry boss who's more focused on his/her next career move than helping the team get better. I focus on the demotivation we experience when we shut off our seeking systems—the part of our brains that craves exploration and learning and that gives us hits of dopamine when we follow its urges.

The seeking system gets activated by three things: encouraging people to (a) play to their strengths, (b) experiment and learn, and (c) feel a sense of purpose.

These three ingredients are often missing in the recipe of large organizations. I don't think most leaders are evil and I don't think most leaders try to squash people's souls. But I do think most leaders have been trained for—and are rewarded for—efficiency and predictability. So organizations have metrics and controls and policies to standardize employee behaviors, and to punish employees when they haven't done what was expected.

In general, this makes us feel standardized and processed as we spend most of our awake hours pursuing repetitive tasks that feel a bit disconnected from the bigger picture. We find ourselves disengaging from these sorts of environments. The worldwide polls show that about 70% of employees are not engaged with their work, and 17% are "actively" disengaged. These are people who are not only unmotivated—they are repelled by what they do all day.

But get this: we're talking about an evolutionary tendency to disengage from tedious activities here. That doesn't sound so bad, does it? Taken out of the modern workplace, it kind of makes sense, right? So low motivation and disengagement from tedious, meaningless tasks isn't some kind of "bug" in our mental makeup. It's a feature. It's our body's way of telling us that we were designed do better things—to keep exploring and learning. This is our biology. It's part of our adaptive unconscious to know that our human potential is being wasted.

Duncan: *Your research shows that many people suffer from "learned help-lessness." Exactly what is that, and how is it manifested in the workplace?*

Cable: Many employees find themselves caught in a crossfire between their biological seeking systems and their organizational realities. Their built-in biology urges them to explore their environments, experiment and learn, and assign meaning. But most people work in organizations where they don't feel that it is possible to do any of these things. After being shut down and punished a few times for using creativity instead of following the rules, employees begin to ignore the urges of their seeking systems. This means they shut off the dopamine and learn to shut down and just "take it." They end up making a living but not a life.

Learned helplessness manifests itself in negative emotional states. We grow resigned and it lowers our motivation. When we learn helplessness, we no longer even try.

Duncan: *What kind of environment is most likely to motivate people to share ideas, work smarter, and embrace change?*

Cable: The positive emotions that emerge from an activated seeking system (curiosity, excitement, zest) are functional in triggering exploration, innovation and positive relationships with others. These emotions have downstream organizational implications such as releasing employee energy, enthusiasm, and creativity. For example, as curiosity and excitement increase, so does creative problem solving, because people are better able to marshal their cognitive resources to cope with the task at hand instead of being encumbered by fear and threat.

Duncan: *What role does a leader's personal humility (or lack of it) play in helping people become and stay engaged in their work?*

Cable: To prompt employees' curiosity, self-expression, and learning through experimentation, a leader can start with the humble purpose of serving others and being open to learning from employees. Research shows that when leaders express humility and share their own developmental journeys, they end up encouraging a learning mindset in others. Ironically, humble leadership works not by demanding perfection, but its opposite—by showing that humans are never perfect and must explore, fail, and practice in order to learn and improve.

For example, some medical teams did not adopt a new method of open-heart surgery, even though it was safer, less invasive and painful, and improved recovery time. The new procedure, which involved special equipment to access the heart through an incision between the ribs, was a source of anxiety. For "God-Complex" know-it-all doctors, the new procedure presented the chance of failure. They did not want to give up power to serve their full team, including nurses. Even though the new approach was better for patients, many doctors continued with the old approach, and lost relevance.

Personal application:

- Be honest. Do you ever suffer from "learned helplessness" at work? If so, what can you do to offset that condition with a more can-do approach to your job?

- What can you do to help create a work environment that's encouraging and uplifting to people?

- How can you do a better job of serving others, regardless of where they are on the organization chart?

24

Close Encounters: Leadership and Handwritten Notes

Commentary: Rodger Dean Duncan

Expert: Doug Conant, former CEO of Campbell Soup Company, co-author of *TouchPoints: Creating Powerful Leadership Connections in the Smallest of Moments*

What you'll learn: By using the "TouchPoint" triad, you can make the most of even the briefest interactions with others.

Effective leadership is not confined to grand gestures and high profile public appearances. It can manifest itself in something as simple—and personal—as a handwritten note.

If there were a Hall of Fame in the American food manufacturing industry, Douglas Conant would be in it. He served in senior executive positions at General Mills and Kraft, then as president of Nabisco Foods and as CEO at Campbell Soup Company.

When Conant talks about leadership, he often says "the action is in the interaction." By this he means that leadership is all about showing up in the moment whenever one interacts with others. It means earnestly working to advance the agenda in a constructive way.

"You can't expect an organization to perform at high levels unless people are personally engaged," Conant says. "And they won't be personally engaged unless they believe you (the leader) are personally engaged in trying to make their lives better."

Conant says there are two keys to staying on the message of engagement. The first is to "declare yourself." People aren't mind readers. They can't know what you're thinking unless you tell them. Explicitly. By declaring yourself, you might say something like, "Okay, we're going to make it safe to challenge the status quo. We're going to make it safe to offer opinions that run counter to the current thinking. We're going to have a culture that places real value on fresh ideas."

Conant says a second step to staying on message is to "deliver on your promises." You must hold yourself accountable to the high standards. You must model high standards at every opportunity. You must walk the talk.

As Campbell's CEO, Conant walked the engagement talk in the most literal way. He wore a pedometer on his belt, and sometime during each day—whether at the headquarters building in New Jersey or at a production plant in Europe or Asia—he put on a pair of walking shoes. His goal was to log 10,000 steps a day (great for the heart!) and to interact meaningfully with as many employees as possible.

"This practice showed people I was paying attention, that I was 'all in,'" Conant says. These brief encounters had multiple benefits. They helped Conant stay informed with the goings-on throughout the company, and to connect personally with people at every level. They enabled people to put a human face on the company's strategy and direction. And they enabled Conant to help celebrate the thousands of little successes that add up to big differences.

In addition to putting in lots of steps, Conant did something else that's unusual for a CEO. He hand-wrote up to 20 notes a day to employees celebrating their successes and contributions. "In my line of work I've been trained to find the busted number in a spreadsheet and identify things that are going wrong," he says. "Most cultures don't do a good job of celebrating contributions. So I developed the practice of writing notes to our employees."

Over ten years, it amounted to more than 30,000 notes, and Campbell had only 20,000 employees. Wherever Conant went in the world, in employee cubicles you'd find his handwritten notes posted on their bulletin boards. Conant's notes were not gratuitous. They celebrated specific contributions. And because the notes were handwritten, they seemed to be treasured more than an email message might be.

What's the primary point here? Messages matter. Repetition matters. Clarity matters. The "personal touch" matters. In fact, Conant coauthored a bestselling book on the subject. It's entitled *TouchPoints: Creating Powerful Leadership Connections in the Smallest of Moments.*

At a time when the information age has morphed into the interruption age, great leaders like Doug Conant learn to look at daily interactions through a fresh lens. Every interaction—whether it's planned or spontaneous, casual or choreographed, in a conference room or on a factory floor—is an opportunity to exercise change-friendly leadership.

Conant used a simple behavioral model to help operationalize this high engagement philosophy. "Leaders have a bias for action," he says. "When they're listening, it may not feel like they're accomplishing anything. Nothing could be further from the truth."

He recommends what he calls a "TouchPoint Triad." In music,

a triad describes the three tones needed to form a complete chord, the three notes that create the harmony. Likewise, Conant says, the "TouchPoint Triad" describes the three key notes needed in even the briefest interactions: (1) Listen Intently, (2) Frame the Issue, and (3) Advance the Agenda.

To "Listen Intently" is all about bringing a "how can I help?" mentality to the discussion and earnestly trying to understand the situation. To "Frame the Issue" is about making sure you understand who owns the issue and what the expectations are of you in the interaction. Finally, to "Advance the Agenda" is about looking for some way to move things forward in the moment.

Over time, this disciplined approach to conducting interactions can exponentially improve one's effectiveness and efficiency, systematically helping to raise one's leadership profile.

Personal application:

- When, and with whom, can you make good use of the "Touch-Point Triad" recommended by Doug Conant?

- You may not be able to write 30,000 personal notes, but exactly what *can* you do demonstrate genuine empathy and connection with your co-workers?

- What do you think would be the effect if you brought more of a "how can I help?" mentality to your relationship with people who report to you?

Feedback and Accountability

"Accountability
breeds
response-ability."

Stephen R. Covey

25

Is There An Elephant in the Room? Name It and Tame It

Commentary: Rodger Dean Duncan

What you'll learn: "Undiscussable" subjects or behaviors can be deadly to a work environment. Follow these suggestions and you won't have to suffer in silence.

Of all the things leaders do, talking is among the most visible and certainly among the most influential. Think about it. You don't add your greatest value by virtue of your skill in manipulating project management software or flipping switches or turning valves. You add your greatest value by interacting with other human beings, and you do that primarily by talking.

It's amazing how many books have been written on the subject of talking. While most of them contribute to the discussion, their essence can be summed up simply: We are most effective when we talk so other people will listen *and* when we listen so other people will talk.

Because it requires honesty and clarity, true dialogue can be uncomfortable. And because people like to avoid discomfort, it's tempting to allow some topics to remain unaddressed—sort of like leaving a splinter in your finger even though logic tells you the temporary pain of digging it out is not nearly as bad as the likely infection from leaving it in.

Most of us have been in situations where there's a relevant issue that nobody seems willing to talk about. We might even say to ourselves, "There's an elephant in this room, and I sure wish someone else would tame that animal." Well, to tame an elephant—an "undiscussable"— you must first acknowledge its existence.

A natural consequence of undiscussables in a culture is that fresh viewpoints get deflected, or even smothered. That's contrary to the whole purpose of dialogue, and dangerous for any organization interested in vitality and achievement.

Our recent (as well as remote) history is replete with examples of intolerance for facts that disturb the status quo.

- At NASA, insulation foam falling off fuel tanks and hitting space shuttles became an undiscussable.

- For Detroit automakers, the marketplace surge of Japanese cars was an undiscussable.

- At IBM, Apple was an undiscussable.

- At American Airlines, cross-state rival Southwest Airlines was an undiscussable.

- At Kodak, digital photography was an undiscussable.

- In the music industry, MP3 file-sharing was an undiscussable.

- Among Michael Jackson's entourage of hangers-on, the pop star's drug dependence was an undiscussable.

You can make your own list. Some organizations harbor veritable herds of unnamed, untamed elephants.

After completing a culture assessment for a major corporation I was doing my "What? So what? and Now what?" presentation to the senior management team. That's where I describe the results, point out the implications of the findings, and make recommendations for change. One of the findings was that the CEO had a shoot-the-messenger reputation that was stifling open dialogue on key operational issues.

In sharing some of the open-ended comments from the survey, I put up a slide with a direct quote from one of the anonymous respondents: "I would love to share my ideas with [the CEO], but it's not safe to speak your mind around here. All he seems to want is a bunch of yes-men."

Within a nanosecond of reading that comment the CEO slammed his fist on the table and shouted "That's ridiculous! Find out who said that and usher him out the door! We don't have room in this organization for people who are too weak-kneed to speak up." All the other executives sort of cowered in silence at this display of fury. Then I simply said: "I. Rest. My. Case." After a long pause the CEO smiled, then chuckled, then broke into a hearty laugh.

The elephant in the room (the CEO's bullying style) had been identified, and now the CEO and his team (and later others) were ready to discuss the undiscussable. They were finally on their way to taming the elephant. And taming that elephant led to identifying and taming others.

Effective leaders understand the difference between *implicit* and *explicit* communication. The elephant—an undiscussable subject—is implicit. It's latent, tacit, undeclared, unexpressed. People talk *around* the elephant without acknowledging that it's in the room and affecting everything that's going on. But until the elephant's presence is made explicit—plain, clear, straightforward, obvious—the quality of true dialogue is limited. Naming and taming the elephant is a metaphor for making implicit issues explicit.

In practicing dialogue, we must be constantly alert to clues that someone may be passively accepting an idea or decision without communicating his true feelings about it. This requires focus. In our natural tendency to avoid resistance, we sometimes hear what we *want* to hear. In reality, we can often learn as much from what is not said as from what is.

Some people hesitate in speaking up to avoid being ostracized or being viewed as "not a team player." An individual's private apprehension at being regarded as different is often more influential on his behavior than actual group pressure.

Undiscussables can easily become the fabric of individual relationships and organizational culture. It works something like this:

- People craft messages (expressed in words and/or behaviors) that contain inconsistencies. For example, "integrity" and "accountability" may be professed values, yet team members frequently miss production deadlines and nobody raises an eyebrow.

- Team members act as if the messages are not inconsistent.

- Team members treat the ambiguity and inconsistency as undiscussable.

- Team members make the undiscussability of the undiscussable also undiscussable.

Taming elephants is a three-part process:

First, identify the elephant. An old proverb says that the beginning of wisdom is to call things by their right names. Although you always want to be respectful, identifying the elephant is not the time to mince words. Call the elephant what it is. In the case of the CEO with the "my way or the highway" leadership approach, referring to his style as merely "tough minded" would have missed the mark and might even have been accepted as a compliment. I told him he was widely regarded as a bully and that his style was having the unintended consequence of shutting down the very kind of straight talk he said he expected of his people.

Second, uncover the underlying assumptions that people have about the elephant. In a spirit of genuine curiosity and discovery, talk openly about your view of the "elephant" and invite the other dialogue participants to share their perspectives. You will be enlightened, and possibly even surprised, by the ways people have constructed their versions of "reality."

Third, make it safe to talk openly about the elephant. People are afraid of elephants because they don't want to get stomped on. Good dialogue skills like listening with empathy and inquiring to discover can help create an atmosphere of acceptance so people can deal openly with their concerns. Underscore the mutual interests you share with the other players.

This is also an important time for participants to relinquish power. Position and status differences have a major effect on people's readiness to explore different points of view honestly.

When I called out the CEO on his bullying tactics, he was mature and professional enough to accept the blunt assessment gracefully. He invited his team to give him examples of where his style had stymied open discussion, assured them his request was genuine, and promised there would no recrimination. This opened the floodgates of some breakthrough feedback and set the stage for candid dialogue on future occasions as well.

Personal application:

- What are some undiscussables in your workplace?
- What effect does ignoring the undiscussables have on morale and overall performance?
- How can you use the principles and practices discuss here to address the undiscussables in a productive way?

26

5 Steps to Feedback That Can Help You Get Better

Commentary: Rodger Dean Duncan

What you'll learn: You do yourself a huge favor when you create an environment where people feel comfortable giving you honest, unvarnished feedback.

There's no doubt about it: feedback is the breakfast of champions.

Top performers *are* top performers because they consistently search for ways to make their best even better. For top performers, "continuous improvement" is not just a glib slogan. It's a mantra with real meaning.

Top performers know that the main thing is to keep the main thing the main thing. For them, the "main thing" is excellent performance.

Top performers are not only good at accepting feedback, they deliberately seek feedback. And they know that feedback is helpful only when it highlights vulnerabilities as well as strengths.

In many professional circles, "peer review" is used to help maintain high standards of performance. Physicians use a form of peer review to certify doctors in special disciplines. Lawyers use a form of peer review, as do academics and others. Many industries, such as nuclear power, have exceptionally rigorous protocols in their peer reviews.

The best leaders I've observed are very good about providing unvarnished feedback on the performance of others. Their feedback is specific and relevant.

At the same time—and this is a key differentiator—the best leaders I know frequently solicit feedback on *their own* performance. They are open to critiques of both their ideas and of their leadership. On occasion, they actively seek "negative" feedback, valuing the voice of counter thinking. (By contrast, less effective leaders—if they solicit feedback at all—most often solicit confirming feedback.)

The most effective leaders I know are careful to break through the information quarantine that sometimes surrounds them. They actively seek negative feedback as well as positive. They understand that in order to perform better they need a full range of information—even when the information doesn't feel good to hear.

Sometimes familiarity—in a situation or relationship—can lull us into assuming we understand something that we really don't. Here's an example.

One summer my wife and I were on a drive. It was a hot day and I stopped at a convenience store. I returned to the car with two bottles of cold water and two Snickers candy bars. My wife thanked me for the water and said it was thoughtful of me to be concerned for her thirst.

"And did you notice that I bought your favorite candy bar?" I asked. To which she replied: "Honey, Snickers is *your* favorite candy bar. I'm not fond of peanuts so I've never cared for Snickers. My favorite candy bar is Milky Way."

So here I was—married to a wonderful woman for several decades—and I somehow never noticed that her favorite candy bar was not the same as *my* favorite.

Think how easy it must be to miss the cues and clues from the people we serve. Are we providing what they really need? Are we really reaching them? Are we really lifting them?

5 Steps To Meaningful Feedback

Here are some simple steps to receiving feedback that can really make a difference for you.

1. Ask. This may seem obvious, but it's amazing how many well-intended people never think to solicit feedback. Make it explicitly clear to your people that you're genuinely interested in their perspectives on how and what you're doing. If you're not accustomed to asking, they're probably not very accustomed to telling. So you need to ask.

2. Listen. Carefully listen—not just with your ears, but with your eyes and with all your body language. Your entire demeanor should say "I care about what you're saying. Most importantly, I care about *you*." Listen to learn and to understand, not to rebut.

3. Ask some more. If someone says you "did a good job" on your presentation, ask for more detail. Was it the story you used to illustrate a key point? Was it the way you handled the questions? Was it that killer PowerPoint you used? Exactly what was it that made for "a good job" on the presentation? And whether the feedback is "positive" or "negative," ask what you can do better next time. Some of the most effective leaders I know go out of their way to solicit feedback from people who are several rungs lower on the organizational ladder.

4. Resist the urge to judge. What if someone said you come across as inaccessible? If you argue against that viewpoint, you're merely providing evidence of its validity. Remember, when you ask for someone's opinion, respect their right to hold that opinion. If someone says you seem aloof, you have a couple of options. You can either act as though you don't care (thereby proving the point) or you can acknowledge that coming across as aloof would certainly harm your effectiveness and ask them for more specifics so you can adjust your behavior. Which of these options do you think might be more helpful?

5. Say thanks. Wouldn't you say thanks if someone presented you with a birthday or holiday gift? Honest, heartfelt feedback is a gift. Acknowledge it as such. In fact, you might even consider saying something like "Your candid feedback is really a gift and I appreciate it. Thanks for your thoughtfulness."

Sometimes our best coaches are the very people we've been asked to serve. It's not called "servant leadership" for nothing.

Personal application:

- Who are the people in your life who are most important to your personal and professional success?

- If they were to give you honest, unvarnished feedback, what kind of blind spots might you be able to discover and avoid?

- How, and when, will you use the suggestions offered here in soliciting, accepting, and using honest feedback?

27

How to Say 'No!'
Without Getting Fired

Expert: Ira Chaleff, executive coach, author of *The Courageous Follower* and *Intelligent Disobedience*.

What you'll learn: Sometimes in your career you'll need to say "no." Knowing how to do it can save both your reputation and your job.

In the early 1970s I worked for a prominent company on Wall Street. I was asked to engage in a practice that, although not illegal, I regarded as clearly unethical.

I pushed back by pointing out that I was successful in my work without using the questionable practice. While acknowledging that was true, my boss told me that in order to advance in the company I would need to teach the practice to others. I couldn't get him to see the disconnect: Why would I be willing to teach others a practice that I regarded as wrong?

We were at a stalemate. So I quit. It was a scary time. I had a wife, a 2-year-old, a newborn baby, and no job. The good news is that this decision was a springboard to professional opportunities I'd never dreamed possible.

Not every situation like this has such a happy ending.

Executive coach Ira Chaleff offers some excellent counsel in his book *Intelligent Disobedience: Doing Right When You're Told to Do Wrong.*

Chaleff uses the metaphor of the guide dog. If a blind man inadvertently walks too close to the edge of a train platform, his guide dog will pull him decisively away from it. This is known as a "counter-pull." It might be a good term to use when a leader is about to step off the edge into unknown danger.

There are ways to say "no" without being insubordinate. In fact, smart leaders and smart followers adopt practices that enable honest conversations to navigate their relationships.

To explore some of those practices, I talked with Ira Chaleff.

Rodger Dean Duncan: *What's the best way to say no to a directive you* *regard as wrong (dangerous, duplicitous, unlawful, immoral, etc.) without coming across as insubordinate?*

Ira Chaleff: First, let me emphasize that not all orders to which we should say "no" are ethical matters. Often a senior executive will issue an order before having the full picture, not realizing that the order is incorrect for the current situation. It's the responsibility of those receiving the order to fill in the correct picture and save the executive from making an expensive or embarrassing mistake.

Regardless if the matter is ethical, operational, or a matter of public image, it can be difficult to get the executive to give it the attention it deserves. They are focused on priorities that have a large impact on the future of the company and resist distractions. This is why those around executives need to develop the art of getting their attention *before* trying to correct their information.

You do this by linking the matter to what is already important to them. If shareholder value is their top concern you might say "There's something I need to inform you about that could impact shareholder value." Once you have their attention you can say why you should not do what was just ordered and present an alternative suggestion.

Duncan: *How can a leader encourage intelligent disobedience without undermining the need for compliance and order in the workplace?*

Chaleff: There is no dichotomy between intelligent disobedience and the need for compliance and order. The operative word is "intelligent."

Intelligent Disobedience is the term used in training guide dogs for people who are blind. After the dog learns how to obey all the commands it needs to support the individual, it is taught how to disobey if obeying would result in harm to the team of human and dog. That is exactly what leaders need from their own teams. Leaders can inadvertently create a climate that does not encourage intelligent disobedience, in which case they put themselves and the organization at risk.

One strategy is for leaders to always present their ideas as first drafts instead of immutable orders and ask "Am I missing anything?" When team members answer this question candidly the leader must resist the inclination to defend his or her draft. Instead, be genuinely curious. Ask follow up questions to help build an understanding of what team members see that you don't. This prevents issuing dangerous orders in the first place.

Duncan: *How can parents and teachers use the principles of intelligent disobedience to help children protect themselves from people who might do them harm?*

Chaleff: My research on the dangers of blind obedience took me into the way children are socialized in the educational system. There is tremendous emphasis in schools on having children know and obey the rules and do what they are told by teachers, administrators, coaches, etc. This programming then extends to all their relationships with authority. While abuse of these positions is rare, when it occurs it can be devastating.

The antidote is a little bit of age appropriate practice in intelligent disobedience. Many parents already tell their kids not to get into cars with strangers. Extend this type of awareness to known authority figures. Set up a role play of what to do if the coach tells you to intentionally hurt the opposing team or if the camp counselor tells you to touch him in ways that make you uncomfortable. This is like doing fire drills even though you hope there is never a fire.

Duncan: *What's the key to maintaining an appropriate balance between respect for an authority figure and knowing when it's time to disobey?*

Chaleff: The key is to hold yourself accountable and never think it is okay to say "I was just following orders." If what you are being told to do is likely to result in harm, it is your responsibility to speak up and, if necessary, to disobey. It may be difficult to do this. It's often more difficult to live with the consequences of having followed a bad order.

Duncan: *Many people have no particular problem identifying when an authority figure's directive violates their conscience. But then they don't know how to push back without jeopardizing the relationship. What's your advice?*

Chaleff: Speaking up may jeopardize the relationship and you may need to do so anyway. There are a number of ways to speak up while minimizing the risk of causing damage. A key element is to find a time to speak without publicly embarrassing the authority and by being clear that you are not rejecting their authority, just the problematic order. If at all possible do this face to face where you can see and respond to reactions, which you cannot do in an email or text message.

There are a range of voices one should know and be able to move between. Often you can start with a diplomatic voice: "I see why you would ask that. Here's another way to achieve this with less risk." You also need to be able to use an assertive voice when warranted. "I can't support that as it poses ethical problems and significant risk to you and the company. Here is what I *can* do."

Personal application:

- What are some of the "little compromises" in your workplace that deserve the attention of an honest and courageous person like you?

- What can you do to encourage others to practice "intelligent disobedience" when working with you?

- How can you hold yourself accountable to high standards in a way that other people will notice but will not cause you to come across as self-righteous?

28

Leadership As Dialogue, Not Monologue

Expert: Jim Kouzes, co-author of *The Leadership Challenge*, named as one of the best executive educators in the U.S.

What you'll learn: Effective leadership is based on genuine empathy for other people's feelings, opinions, and circumstances. Mutual understanding is a critical ingredient.

You may have excellent technical skills. You may even be innovative and visionary. But if you don't know how to *engage* people, you're toast.

The best leaders (regardless of title or lack thereof) have good people skills. They talk well. They listen well. They offer feedback in ways that inspire improvement rather than resistance. They welcome feedback, and accept it without excuses.

To explore these all-important behaviors, I visited with Jim Kouzes, the Dean's Executive Fellow of Leadership at Santa Clara University.

With his colleague Barry Posner, Kouzes is co-author of the internationally award-winning and bestselling book *The Leadership Challenge* (with upwards of three million copies sold). They've co-authored more than 30 other books, including *The Truth About Leadership, Credibility, Encouraging the Heart,* and *A Leader's Legacy. The Wall Street Journal* named Kouzes as one of the ten best executive educators in the U.S., and he's been recognized as one of *HR Magazine's* Top 20 Most Influential International Thinkers.

Rodger Dean Duncan: *In your practice you often make the point that leadership is a dialogue, not a monologue. How does dialogue inspire a shared vision and enable others to act?*

Jim Kouzes: Leadership is about relationships, and strong relationships are built on mutual understanding. You can get to that *mutual* understanding only through conversation and dialogue.

This means you can't adopt the view that visions come from the top down. You have to start engaging others in a collective dialogue about the future, not delivering a monologue. You can't mobilize people to willingly travel to places they don't want to go. No matter how grand the dream of an individual visionary, if others don't see in it the possibility of realizing their hopes and desires, they won't follow voluntarily or wholeheartedly.

To become an exemplary leader, you must develop a deep appreciation of the collective hopes, dreams, and aspirations of your constituents. Constituents come to believe in their leaders—to see them as worthy of their trust—when they believe that the leaders have the constituents' best interests at heart.

Duncan: *Genuine empathy is essential.*

Kouzes: Absolutely. Leaders who are clearly interested only in their own agendas, their own advancement, and their own wellbeing will not be followed willingly. You have to reach out and attend to others, be present with them, and listen to them.

This isn't just theory. We know from our research that when leaders seek consensus around shared values, constituents are more positive. People who report that their managers engage in dialogue regarding common values feel a significantly stronger sense of personal effectiveness than individuals who feel that they're wasting energy trying to figure out what they're supposed to be doing.

Duncan: *What else does good dialogue bring to relationships?*

Kouzes: Dialogue also produces clarity. One study, for example, reported 185 different behavioral expectations about the value of "integrity" alone. Even with commonly identified values, there may be little agreement on the meaning of the values statements.

The lesson here is that leaders must engage their constituents in conversation about matters of principle. A common understanding of values emerges from a process, not a pronouncement.

Duncan: *So dialogue helps produce a sense of community?*

Kouzes: Exactly. Exemplary leaders also know that they can't do it alone. Nothing extraordinary ever happened without the enthusiastic and committed involvement of others. Leadership is not a solo performance. It's a team effort. Leaders need partners to make extraordinary things happen in organizations.

Therefore, effective leaders invest in creating trustworthy relationships. They build spirited and cohesive teams, teams that feel like family. They actively involve others in planning and give them the discretion to make their own decisions. Leaders make others feel like owners, not hired hands.

Leaders develop collaborative goals and cooperative relationships with colleagues. They are considerate of the needs and interests of others. They know that these relationships are the keys that unlock support. Leaders bring people together, creating an atmosphere understanding and a shared fate. Mutual respect is what sustains extraordinary group efforts.

Duncan: *To help people clarify their strengths and identify opportunities for improvement, 360-degree feedback is often used in leadership training and coaching. What advice do you have for people who resist participating in such a feedback process?*

Kouzes: The truth is that the best leaders are the best learners. We find in our research that higher performing leaders more frequently engage in learning activities than do lower performing leaders.

Feedback is at the center of any learning process. Without feedback there is no learning. Thoughtfully studying feedback on your performance is the only way for you to know whether you're getting close to your goal and whether you're executing properly. Researchers consistently point out that the development of expertise or mastery requires one to receive constructive, even critical, feedback.

People need to know if they're making progress toward the goal or simply marking time. People's motivation to perform a task increases only when they have a challenging goal *and* receive feedback on their progress.

Goals without feedback, or feedback without goals, have little effect on people's willingness to put extra effort (or motivation) into the task. Just announcing that the idea is to reach the summit is not enough to get people to put forth more effort. They need information on whether they're still climbing in the right direction, making progress toward the top, or sliding downhill.

With clear goals and detailed feedback, people can become self-correcting and can more easily understand their place in the big picture.

Duncan: *So you agree that feedback directly influences the amount of effort a person invests in self-improvement?*

Kouzes: Absolutely. For example, consider what happens to your self-confidence without feedback. In a study, people were told that their efforts would be compared with how well hundreds of others had done on the same task. They received praise, criticism, or no feedback on their performance. Those who heard nothing about how well they did suffered as great a blow to their self-confidence as those who were criticized. Only those who received positive feedback improved.

However, our studies on exemplary leadership consistently show that the statement receiving the lowest rating, both from leaders as well as their constituents, is "Asks for feedback on how his/her actions affect other people's performance." In other words, the behavior that leaders and their constituents consider to be the weakest is the behavior that most enables leaders to know how they're doing!

You can't learn very much if you're unwilling to find out more about the impact of your behavior on the performance of those around you. It's your responsibility as a leader to keep asking others, "How am I doing?" If you don't ask, they're not likely to tell you.

Duncan: *What can be done to create a "feedback-friendly" environment, and what are the characteristics of helpful feedback?*

Kouzes: It's not always easy to get feedback. It's not generally asked for, and most people aren't used to providing it. Skills are required to do both. You can increase the likelihood that people will accept honest feedback from you if you make it easier for people to give honest feedback to you. To be most effective, good feedback needs to be specific, not general. It must be focused on behavior, not on the individual (personality). It should be solicited rather than imposed. It should be timely rather than delayed. And it should be descriptive rather than evaluative. You must be sincere in your desire to improve yourself, and you must demonstrate that you are open to knowing how others see you.

Personal application:

- In interacting with the people you lead, under what circumstances might you be tempted to engage in a monologue rather than dialogue?

- What specific steps can you take to help create a "feedback-friendly" environment in your workplace?

Communication

"If you just communicate,
you can get by. But if you
communicate skillfully,
you can work miracles."

29

Hit the Bullseye With Your Communication

Expert: G. Riley Mills, noted communication coach, co-author of *The Pin Drop Principle* and *The Bullseye Principle*

What you'll learn: Most of your communication is routine, but some of it is genuinely high stakes. Following a simple framework can help you excel with your messaging.

Most people can talk. But then they risk assuming that uttering words is the same as communication. It's not.

Genuine communication is much more than merely expressing an opinion or dumping information. It's all about connecting: connecting with people's hopes, dreams, values, concerns.

Multiple studies show that effective communication skills are at the heart of personal and professional success. Technical skills are fine, but if you can't "connect" with other people you're at a distinct disadvantage. The good news is that you can get better.

That's the essence of *The Bullseye Principle*, a definitive guide for anyone wanting to excel with high-stakes conversations, presentations, and collaborations.

Co-author G. Riley Mills, a seasoned communication coach, shares some ideas that can help boost your ability to influence.

Rodger Dean Duncan: *There's no doubt that the ability to communicate with purpose and clarity is a critical key to personal and professional success. You take that truism a step further by emphasizing what you call "intention-based communication." What exactly is that?*

G. Riley Mills: Intention-based communication applies to business communication the same techniques actors and world leaders have used for centuries to appear confident, credible, and compelling.

The goal of intention-based communication is to ensure your audience understands why your message is important to them through your delivery—*how* you say it.

To use an analogy, we view communication like an arrow whizzing through the air to its target. The target's bullseye is your objective—what you want your audience to think/feel/do after hearing your message. The arrow is your message. Your intention is how you launch the arrow.

Intention is a strong one-word descriptor. In practical terms, if you want to excite, motivate, or inspire your audience, your intention must be congruent with your message and your audience should clearly see excite, motivate, or inspire in all areas of your communication—body language, word choices, facial expressions, and vocal dynamics.

Without a strong, clear intention, your message will be ambiguous at best.

Duncan: *You cite a study showing that 62% of young workers believed their oral communication skills are good enough for them to succeed at work, while only 28% of their employers agree. Why the difference in perception? Why are young people so over-confident in this regard?*

Mills: Young workers aren't the only group assuming their communication skills are up to par. Business professionals of all ages and job responsibilities can benefit from improving their communication skills.

The perception gap between employers and younger worker's communication skills is complex. Boomers typically communicate in-person while younger workers prefer instant messaging, text and email. Young workers assume multiple internships have adequately prepared them for the workforce. But they haven't. Young workers assume companies are more interested in hard skills than soft skills. But they aren't. And schools at all levels aren't adequately preparing young workers with the communication skills needed to succeed in the workplace.

The biggest communication skills gap though, across all ages, is we assume because we talk everyday, we must be good communicators. Effective communication, though, like any skill, takes time and focused practice.

Duncan: *In the business world there's a lot of hand-wringing about low levels of employee engagement. What role can or should communication play in boosting engagement?*

Mills: To increase employee engagement, improve your manager's communication skills. We know people leave companies because of their managers, and the data show how managers affect the bottom line:

- A manager's leadership style is responsible for 30% of a company's bottom-line profitability.

- One study showed that 70% of the variance in the employee engagement of teams could be traced back to the influence of the manager.
- Employees were three times more likely to be engaged if managers held regular meetings with their direct reports.

Duncan: *In this modern age of 140-character tweets, what helpful lessons can people learn from Aristotle's writings from more than 2,000 years ago?*

Mills: The biggest lesson is, regardless of platform—in person, conference call, email, twitter, etc.—communication can be distilled to the same three elements: Speaker. Subject. Audience.

As Aristotle pointed out, we are all just speakers communicating a message to an audience. That means, regardless of medium, you must constantly go back to the first step in our 3-step process for influential communication: *analyzing your audience.* If communication is meant to influence another person's behavior, it must be grounded in the receiver's desires and interests.

Aristotle's three means of persuasion—ethos, logos, pathos—are still a good guide for anyone communicating information today. To best influence an audience, no matter the industry or subject, you benefit from being seen as sincere, credible and passionate as a leader or executive.

Duncan: *Before any communication—whether offering a comment in a meeting or launching a major promotion campaign—what are three questions that should be addressed?*

Mills: We all want something as a result of our communication. And the clearer the message, the easier it is to hit the bullseye and get what we want. You must know whom you are talking to. How can you satisfy the needs of your audience and customize your message for them if you don't know who they are?

The first step is to analyze your audience. Consider demographic, psychographic, and situational factors:

- *Demographic*—age, marital status, gender, education level, occupation, religion as well as cultural, racial, and ethnic backgrounds.
- *Psychographic*—attitudes, beliefs, values, loyalties, pre-conceived notions, feelings, and level of knowledge of your topic.
- *Situational*—size of group, time of meeting, occasion, event's length, room size and, seating arrangement.

The second step is understand the reaction your message should elicit—how you want them to feel and, subsequently, what you want them to do as a result of hearing your message (your objective).

The third step is to modify your delivery to achieve that result—modifying how you say what you say to accomplish your objective.

Duncan: *It's been said that marketing is less about what you make than about the stories you tell. What's the best formula for an effective organizational narrative?*

Mills: We recommend applying the dramatic structure developed by Gustav Freytag, a 19th century German novelist, to business storytelling. It's the same framework for effective storytelling that novelists, playwrights, and screenwriters use.

- *Establish background information (exposition).* Who is the story about, when and where does it take place? The more descriptive, the better the picture you will paint for your audience.
- *Identify the problem (inciting incident).* Develop conflict. Introduce the pain point or problem. What incident or event gets the ball rolling? Who what is the villain?
- *Detail the solution (rising action).* Build and reveal pertinent information to drive the story forward. Show steps taken to address the problem and clearly identify a solution.
- *Spotlight the result (climax).* Describe specifically how you did it and how you achieved a positive outcome. Focus on the benefit your solution provided and ensure the story's climax aligns directly with your objective for telling the story.
- *State the takeaway (falling action and resolution).* Wrap up your story with a one or two line closing that clearly defines what the listener should have learned from your story.

We all have stories we can share to inspire or enlighten others. Your job as a storyteller is to kick off the story and get to the ending in the fastest, most interesting way possible. And remember, in most cases, a story is always about the ending—the lesson or moral you want to drive home.

Personal application:

- How can you use the principles of intention-based communication in your next meeting? In your next presentation?

- Select a typical workday during the next week or so. During that day, keep track of how much time you invest in interacting with others (beyond routine chit chat.) Now, ask yourself what you can do to be more effective in your communication by applying the storytelling framework discussed here.

30

Tap the Power of Storytelling

Expert: Geoffrey Berwind, communication consultant, coach to dozens of TEDx speakers

What you'll learn: The sweet spot of effective communication is a good story. Hone your storytelling skills and people will sit up and listen.

No doubt about it, the best speakers are good storytellers. The best writers are good storytellers. The best leaders are good storytellers. The best teachers and trainers and coaches are good storytellers. It might even be argued that the best parents are good storytellers.

While storytelling is not the only way to engage people with your ideas, it's certainly a critical part of the recipe.

My friend Geoffrey Berwind is a professional storytelling consultant and trainer. He's created storytelling projects for historic sites and provides consulting services for leaders, entrepreneurs, speakers, and companies worldwide. His clients include Historic Philadelphia, Inc., Kennedy Space Center Visitor Complex, UNUM Global IT Leaders, along with thousands of experts in many fields who want to make a deeper impact on their audiences, customers, management teams, and influential stakeholders. Geoffrey has also trained dozens of speaker to achieve their TEDx talks.

I invited Geoffrey to share some of what he's learned about the power of good storytelling.

Rodger Dean Duncan: *Why is there so much buzz about the use of Story in business communications?*

Geoffrey Berwind: For too long, companies have relied on offering change ideas only by supplying data, numbers, statistics, analytics, and so on. We've heard for years now that "PowerPoint is dead," yet time and again this is the expected form of communicating an idea or proposal. Steve Jobs was one of the pioneers in the use of simple images and one-line concepts to support his verbal storytelling. TED Talks have carried that practice forward and their world-class speakers are expected to speak in simple narratives, using stories and powerful imagery to convey their message.

Because of the overwhelming information saturation and bombardment we are all under, stories provide a powerful counterbalance to the overabundance of analytical, academic, conceptual jargon.

In a TED talk, you're expected to focus on an "idea worth spreading." This short-form talk, which today is an average of 12 minutes, is expected to be what I have described as the "Four C's of a great TED talk." You need to be Concise, Clear, Compelling and Credible. Storytelling is your best way to be Compelling.

Duncan: *Why use stories when speaking in a business setting?*

Berwind: Stories powerfully connect us to our listeners. When we share our own real-life stories or the stories of others (Example or Proof stories) our audiences feel that they get to know us as authentic people – people who have lives outside the corporate setting, people who have struggled with problems and who have figured out how to overcome them.

There's a well-known marketing axiom that "people buy from people they know, like and trust." During my years of training in making presentations I've seen that there is simply no more impactful way to have that occur than through the strategic use of storytelling. Great leaders recognize that human connections need to go before concepts and strategies: connect first with your prospects, your audiences— *then* get down to business. I've seen increased attention being paid by companies to the mastery of these so-called "soft skills."

Duncan: *What role can storytelling play in a speaker's credibility?*

Berwind: How long have humans been around? As long as there have been campfires, humans have gathered around them and conveyed their view of the world through the use of stories. Stories are a "shared experience," and I believe we are hard-wired to receive information primarily through storytelling. Stories trigger the ancient human muscle of the imagination.

Our own early years were largely spent through play and exploring. We experienced the world through direct engagement and, as children, we learned through being told bedtime stories, fairy tales, hearing family stories around the dinner table. We became *story-listeners* when we were young. When leaders use storytelling I believe they bring their audiences back to a natural state of primal listening.

So, credibility isn't really an issue. The use of stories, properly conveyed, is actually how we *prefer* to receive communications. When leaders learn how to meld the use of stories with the left-brain data-based information they also need to convey … well, this becomes irresistible. Their influence and engagement becomes more powerful, and real change occurs because people are moved to action.

Duncan: *What kinds of stories could leaders use to influence others?*

Berwind: There are a number of powerful strategic stories you could use to persuade and influence. A "Purpose Story" is a big picture story that conveys a big idea. Use "Example or Proof Stories" to illustrate how others overcame a similar problem and had a successful outcome. When offering a change-idea, craft a "What If?" or "Imagine …" story.

In your "story toolbox" you can also use Cautionary stories, Teaching stories, Inspirational stories, and your own Everyday stories that make you more relatable to your audiences.

Duncan: *When making a speech, is there an ideal kind of story to begin with?*

Berwind: Many of us feel a sense of mission in life beyond simply making money. Most leaders feel some kind of passion for what they do and so when they convey this they can deeply affect their audiences. If you are offering a change-idea, you're pitching a transformation of some kind—so your goal is to overcome resistance in those who are in front of you. Sharing why you care, why it matters becomes pivotal.

I encourage professionals to craft their Why I Do What I Do story— (which I recommend using at the very beginning of a speech). This WHY is the very heart of why we use stories: before you prescribe the "What," the "Who," the "How" and the "When," be clear about the WHY. It makes all the difference. Tell your stories!

Duncan: *If someone could watch only two or three TED talks as models of excellent storytelling to convey a message, which ones would you recommend?*

Berwind: Three of my favorite TED speakers who use storytelling are Jeff Smith ("Lessons in business...from prison"), Bryan Stevenson ("We need to talk about an injustice"), and Brené Brown ("The Power of Vulnerability").

Personal application:

- Who are the most effective storytellers you know? What is it about their communication that makes their message(s) interesting, compelling, and credible?

- From observing effective storytellers, what lessons can you glean that can be applied to your own communication efforts?

- What is your personal "WHY" story? What effect does that story have on your sense of purpose and meaning in your work?

- Make a list of both your personal and professional pivotal life experiences. Once you do that, identify the ones where your audience or prospects might see themselves in that event. Your goal when you tell stories is to have listeners think to themselves, "me, too."

31

The Art of Persuasion: Why Less Really is More

Expert: Carmine Gallo, communication coach, author of *The Presentation Skills of Steve Jobs* and several other books

What you'll learn: Techniques used by great presenters as disparate as Steve Jobs and Pope Francis.

You have a great idea. It's fresh and innovative. It meets a need. You know it will work.

Your "it" could be a recommendation, a proposal, a design, a procedure, or a tangible product. Whatever your "it" is, you're seriously pumped. Your solution is so awesome people will gasp in wonder. You built it, and surely they will come.

Don't bet on it. Good ideas don't sell themselves.

Venture capitalist Michael Moritz was approached by a couple of Stanford grad students. They were in search of funding for their idea. Moritz had seen a long line of boring PowerPoint presentations and he expected the worst. But to his surprise and delight, the two young guys could summarize their idea in fewer than ten words: "We organize the world's information and make it accessible."

The idea proposed by Larry Page and Sergey Brin was something called Google. The rest is history.

In an age of information overload, good communicators stand above the crowd. But they aren't freaks of nature. They've learned how to persuade and they practice. A lot. They deliver dynamic presentations and share compelling stories that sell products, grow brands, and inspire change.

Communication coach Carmine Gallo sat down with me to discuss some of the learnable practices that top communicators make seem so natural. His latest book is *Five Stars: The Communication Secrets to Get From Good to Great.*

Rodger Dean Duncan: *You make the bold statement that the ability to communicate persuasively is the single greatest skill that will set someone apart in the next decade. Why is this skill so disproportionately critical?*

Carmine Gallo: I didn't come up with the theory. I'm the messenger. It's the opinion of historians, scientists, and business leaders a lot smarter than I am. For example, University of Illinois at Chicago economics professor Deirdre McCloskey says that at least 25% of America's total economy is based on persuasion—changing minds. That's for the total economy, but for business professionals in many categories, persuasion takes up 75% or more of their daily activity.

McCloskey's research has been replicated by economists in other countries. It makes sense. With each technological transformation (agrarian to industrial, industrial to digital), we do less work by hand. The new jobs are in occupations that reward communication, collaboration, and leadership skills. Mastering the art of persuasion is the secret to thriving in the world of automation and artificial intelligence.

Duncan: *Communication skill has always been important, but in today's world of data overload it's more valuable than ever. What effect have social media had on the way we process information?*

Gallo: I consider social media platforms as valuable exercises in learning to communicate more effectively. For example, Twitter gave us the 140-character message. It's since expanded to 280 characters, but I recommend sticking to 140.

Here's a great exercise for anyone with an idea, product, or service to pitch—explain it in a sentence short enough to fit in a Twitter post. In Hollywood pitch meetings, it's called the "logline." A screenwriter must be able to convey the gist of the movie in one sentence.

I've heard the same tactic used in venture capital meetings. An entrepreneur should be able to summarize an idea in one short sentence. Otherwise, it hasn't been thought through.

Duncan: *Neuroscientists say people form an impression about a speaker in as little as 5 to 15 seconds. So how should a speaker handle that all-important first quarter minute?*

Gallo: Like it or not, the research is clear—we make judgments about people before they say a word. First, dress a little better than everybody else in the room (about 25% better). Then, stand straight, give a firm handshake, make eye contact and smile. Research shows that even hardened financial analysts will judge a CEO's perceived competence largely on these nonverbal gestures.

Duncan: *At IT giant Cisco, top leaders believe communication skills are* *the "lubricant of execution" that gives the company its competitive edge. If that's true, why?*

Gallo: Cisco executives provided one of the most fascinating insights I learned in my research. Every manager and executive receives a score for their presentation skills. Although the company doesn't reveal this publicly, it's common knowledge among insiders that people who have below-average or even average communication skills are unlikely to get promoted. That's why it's critical to receive a 4 or a 5 (the maximum score) in every presentation. Five-star persuaders stand out. It doesn't matter if Cisco's data shows its products can outperform competitors. If a sales manager or executive cannot explain it well, they've lost an opportunity to grow the company.

Duncan: *You say storytelling is not a "soft" skill but is the "equivalent of hard cash." What role do stories play in a good communicator's tool kit?*

Gallo: As a writer and journalist, I appreciate the power of story. But during my research, I learned that storytelling is a far more lucrative skill than you might think. At Google, for example, I met a data analyst whose unofficial title is "Chief Storytelling Officer." He conducts workshops to teach Google salespeople data storytelling. Collectively, the salespeople who have taken his class are responsible for billions of dollars in annual revenue. Google has mountains of data that can help customers achieve their business objectives. But if a customer cannot understand how the data will help, it doesn't matter. "Storytelling is a powerful way to get our customers to think differently," he told me. Stories inform, educate and inspire. Storytelling is our best verbal tool to make a heart and mind connection with another person. It works for Google.

Duncan: *Many speakers commit the crime of assault by PowerPoint. What do you recommend for visuals to reinforce a speech or presentation?*

Gallo: I agree with you. Most PowerPoint presentations are an assault on the senses. PowerPoint is not the problem; the problem is the speaker. I've seen marvelous PowerPoint presentations. They're marvelous because they have more pictures than words. The neuroscience literature is clear on this—pictures are superior to text on a slide if you want your audience to recall and act on your idea. Bullet points are the least effective way of transferring information.

I recommend an exercise that I call the "10-40 rule." No more than 40 words in the first ten slides. I learned this trick after studying Steve

Jobs for a book I wrote about his presentation skills. Most slides have 40 words per slide. Jobs didn't reach 40 words until about 10 slides into his presentation. That approach forces you to think about a narrative—the story. It forces you to be more creative.

I also recommend experimenting with different tools. I use Apple Keynote when I have a lot of video because it incorporates video clips seamlessly. I use Prezi when I want to show the relationship between concepts (you can zoom in and out of the presentation and jump around instead being boxed into a linear template). Above all, replace words with pictures as much as possible.

Duncan: *You use Pope Francis as an example of a speaker who effectively employs "the Rule of Three." What exactly is that rule and how does it work?*

Gallo: The rule of three is the most powerful concept in communication theory. It's well established in the research that we can carry only about three or four points in short-term memory. Great writers have known this intuitively for centuries. Thomas Jefferson gave us three unalienable rights—not 18. In popular fables Goldilocks saw three bears, Scrooge saw three ghosts, the hungry wolf encountered three little pigs. You get the idea. Breaking things up into thirds is simply how our brains are wired to mentally categorize information.

Pope Francis has said he learned about the rule of three in seminary. Today, in every major speech and sermon, Francis delivers his ideas in groups of three. In business, give your customer three benefits of the product. Give the hiring manager three reasons to hire you. Give your students three things to remember about the lecture. The rule of three. It's simple and it works.

Duncan: *What can we learn from watching TED talks? What common denominators of communication success should we look and listen for?*

Gallo: TED Talks are the gold standard of public-speaking. There are TED-like elements that everyone should include in their presentations. First, tell more stories. In my research, I found that stories comprised 65% or more of some of the most popular TED talks. Second, don't use bullet points on a slide. Ever. Third, practice more than you ever have.

I spoke to a scientist, Dr. Jill Bolte-Taylor, whose TED talk has been viewed 23 million times. She told me she practiced 400 times. When is the last time you practiced a presentation even 10 times? It's like a champion athlete who visualizes the event for hours or who practices thousands of three-foot putts. When the pressure it on, they rely on muscle memory and their training takes over. It's the same with presentations. The more you practice, the more comfortable you'll feel when the pressure is on.

Personal application:

- Explain your big idea (for a product, process, or something else important to you) in 140 characters or fewer (like a Twitter tweet). What does that exercise tell you about the need for more clarity and precision in your thinking and in your communication?

- Watch five TED talks on a wide range of subjects. What common elements do you notice in the way the speakers deliver their messages? How can you use those observations in your own communication?

- In your next important communication, how can you effectively use the rule of three?

32

Stories: The Effective Leader's Must-Have Tool

Expert: Kevin Cashman, pioneer in the field of CEO and executive development, bestselling author of *Leadership From the Inside Out*

What you'll learn: Research shows that character-driven stories enhance empathy and cooperative behaviors.

Good stories have a power all their own. They can make complex issues understandable. They can give people a sense of community. They can call people to action in ways they never imagined.

As a young journalist many years ago I covered large events ranging from business conventions to religion conferences to political rallies. I always watched and listened to the speakers very carefully. But most revealing was what I observed in the audiences. When a speaker said something like "Let me illustrate with a story," the audience would *always* become more alert and attentive. It was as though the listeners were thinking "Okay, here comes the really good stuff." So why don't more leaders have storytelling in their toolbox of skills? That's always been a mystery to me. But one thing's for sure: the value of good stories and effective storytelling cannot be overemphasized.

Kevin Cashman certainly knows this. In the updated edition of his fine book *Leadership from the Inside Out* he highlights many of the whys and wherefores of good storytelling. He shared some of his insights.

Rodger Dean Duncan: *You say that spreadsheets are the language of management information and stories are the language of leadership inspiration. How can a leader go from mere storytelling skills to using stories to connect people's self-awareness to service and performance improvement? In other words, how can good stories go beyond mere rah-rah and really inspire people to want to improve?*

Kevin Cashman: Numbers are numbing to most people while stories speak to the whole person, both head and heart. Using an authentic, relevant story draws people in, engages our imaginations and our memories so that even if the exact experience didn't happen to us, we feel like it did. It resonates with meaning. So rather than grind through numbers, goals or updates, share a story that illustrates what you value, admire or celebrate in the organization. Research shows that character-driven stories enhance empathy and cooperative behaviors, such as engaging employees to help customers solve problems and feel good about their part in finding a resolution. Telling founding stories connects people to purpose, the original passion behind the enterprise.

Duncan: *How can stories become part of an organization's culture, part of a team's DNA?*

Cashman: Telling founding stories is an excellent way to connect everyone to the original passion behind the enterprise. Keeping that story at the forefront with the organization's purpose and helping individuals connect to it with their own purpose story is a great foundation for an organization's culture.

The privilege of a leader is to inspire new narratives. Recognize that every experience is a potential story that is part of the organization's DNA. People may *already* have a story about you, your team and your organization. The real question is: what is the current story and how do you want to change it?

Duncan: *The sweet spot of an effective story seems to be the intersection of the storyteller's authenticity and the relevant needs of the listeners. How can story mastery be learned and constantly improved?*

Cashman: Effective stories require that we go deep to know our deepest narratives of character, learning, loss, recovery, privilege, and values. This is the journey to authenticity. Relevance requires that we understand the needs, fears, concerns, and struggles of others. Relevance is the journey to emotional intelligence and connection. Story mastery is going deep to touch others. Reflection and connection are key practices throughout these journeys.

Duncan: *How can a leader build up an inventory of authentic stories that engage and inspire others (and even motivate the storyteller)?*
Cashman: Notice that stories, inspiring stories, are already within us and around us. First, know your own stories. Reflect on the highs and lows of your life to inventory your learnings, loss, and values.

Second, begin to notice stories around you, on your team, in your organization, in your family, in your reading, the media … everywhere! Recount these stories to celebrate the character you admire in others.

Know the inventory of stories is already there, but we may not "have taken stock of our story inventory" inside and outside of ourselves.

Duncan: *What are the must-have ingredients of a story that inspires people with a desire to do better and be* better?

Cashman: Ingredient #1: the story moves you. If it is not inspiring to you, it will not inspire others. All inspiration begins with self-inspiration.

Ingredient #2: The story moves others. This involves crafting the narrative in a way that transcends itself and reminds us of a universal challenge, character trait or important consequence. When it does, relevance dawns, inspiration happens and scientists tell us that the hormone, oxytocin, associated with trust and connection, literally flows in our bloodstream!

Personal application:

- In communicating about the challenges and opportunities in your business, how can you replace numbers and other data with stories that engage people's heads, hearts, and hopes?

- What is a good "founding story" that can remind people of the original passion or purpose behind your team or organization?

- What are some good resources for building up a good inventory of relevant stories for your use?

Career Management

"There is no passion to be found playing small – in settling for a life that is less than the one you are capable of living."

Nelson Mandela

33

Don't Quit Your Day Job: Secrets to Finding Work You Really Love

Expert: Jon Acuff, personal development trainer, author of *START: Punch Fear in the Face, Escape Average, Do Work That Matters*

What you'll learn: How to "fall in like" with the job you have so you can prepare for the job you love.

Let's face it. Most adults spend the vast majority of their non-sleeping time at work. Not with their loved ones. Not with their hobbies. Not at the beach building sand castles. At work.

So doesn't it make sense to find work that is truly satisfying?

Jon Acuff, one of today's most compelling voices in the personal development arena, has some good ideas for you. He's the author of two bestselling books on the subjects of work and jobs. His first was *Quitter: Closing the Gap Between Your Day Job & Your Dream Job*. Then came *START: Punch Fear in the Face, Escape Average, Do Work That Matters*.

Let's see if Jon's advice can help in *your* journey to a work life that's more satisfying than ever.

Rodger Dean Duncan: *In previous generations, people often stayed with the same job their entire careers. Today, it's not uncommon to see a brainiac high performer change jobs every three to five years. What are the key differences between a serial quitter and someone who frequently changes jobs for genuinely good reasons?*

Jon Acuff: I think the key difference can be clearly seen by looking at two things: attitude and relationships. The times I was a serial quitter, I ended up getting bitter at the job I was currently at. I didn't jump to a better opportunity, I escaped from what I thought was a bad one. At other times, my jump wasn't driven by my ego or my frustration. It was driven by genuinely good reasons, as you mention, and that made all the difference.

So I tell people: If you're thinking of jumping right now, I dare you to look at your attitude before you do. The second aspect of a good jump versus a serial jump, which sounds like it involves Lucky Charms, is the state of the relationships you leave behind. It's common for there to be hurt feelings whenever you leave a job. That's natural, but did you burn bridges? Is it impossible to ever work with whole groups of people again? Serial quitters tend to leave smoldering bridges behind them.

Duncan: *In assessing what may be a person's "dream job," you recommend using a Magnifying Glass, a Kaleidoscope, and a Telescope. What does that mean?*

Acuff: I recommend that you focus on the telescope approach. Most of the times when we think about jumping to a dream job we look through a magnifying glass or a kaleidoscope.

The magnifying glass blows all our fears up out of proportion as we obsess over worse case scenarios that might never come to fruition.

The kaleidoscope throws all your fears together in a jumbled mess. It's not just about changing jobs, it's about your identity, self worth and entire life.

With a telescope, though, you can see the concerns from a distance. You don't ignore them. You view them for what they are, far off possibilities, and then you plan for them accordingly.

Duncan: *You advise people to "fall in like" with the job they don't love. How does that help move you closer to a job that you do indeed love?*

Acuff: People who are miserable all week have a hard time hustling on the weekend. If you're going to spend 40-50 hours a week doing a job, you set yourself up for failure if you refuse to make it as good as it can be while you're there. It's not about falling in love with it. It might always be a job you only like. That's okay, but don't accept "misery" as the only option you have until you find your dream job.

Sometimes, changing your attitude and expectations about your current job can even help you see there might be a dream job hidden at the company you're already at.

Duncan: *For most people, there's a gap between good intentions and actual performance. What are some behaviors that help close the gap?*

Acuff: Get up early. Watch less TV. Put in the work. The list of possible behaviors is long, but the more time I spend helping people the more I realize one of the biggest keys is having strong relationships.

We need people who will encourage us and challenge us. Fear always tries to put you on an island, as if you're the only one hustling on a certain situation. That's simply not true. Find a friend and be brave enough to be honest that there's a gap between your intentions and your performance. We're not meant to chase dreams alone.

Duncan: *It's possible that a lot of people reading this conversation will demonstrate symptoms of the Yeah-but Syndrome—as in, "Yeah, but that advice doesn't apply to me" or "Yeah, but my situation really is different." What dose of reality can you prescribe?*

Acuff: Those are both fantastic excuses to stay stuck. If none of this advice applies to you, find some advice that does. There are a lot of authors like me writing about this topic. Find one you connect with more.

Just don't be like the young college graduate I met. I asked her, "Who is doing the kind of dream job you'd like to do someday? Who can you learn from?" She said, "No one is doing what I want to do." I immediately thought, "Sure, you went 0 for 6 billion. There's not another human alive who you can learn from." I don't think every bit of advice fits every situation, but I promise there's someone out there who has some you can apply to your career.

Personal application:

- If you're thinking of changing jobs, what careful analysis have you applied to your motives? Are you sure you're not about to burn some bridges?

- How can you use the idea of a magnifying glass, a kaleidoscope, and a telescope in honestly assessing your thinking about a different job?

- If you don't love your current job, what can you do to "fall in like" with it? What could be the advantage of that?

34

If (and When) Your Career Stalls, Reinvent Yourself

Experts: John Hillen and Mark Nevins, co-authors of *What Happens Now? Reinvent Yourself as a Leader Before Your Business Outruns You*

What you'll learn: What got you where you are may not get you where you want (and need) to be.

Has your career stalled? If it hasn't yet, it likely will.

Don't take that personally. Career stalls happen to some of the most capable people in business.

Here's the good news: A career stall doesn't have to be catastrophic. In fact, a temporary career stall can provide the ideal launch pad to a magnificent second or third act.

At one time or another you're likely to face one or more of these common stalls:

1. You can't engage people in your organization's purpose
2. Your team flounders, failing to deliver the desired high performance
3. You lose your influence with key stakeholders
4. You stumble in making a case for important change
5. Your former source of authority slips in the eyes of followers
6. You burn out, losing focus on where and how to invest your time and energy You can't keep your own leader from failing
7. You can't keep your own leader from failing

Rather than hunker down and try to avoid the inevitable career stall, it's best to master a set of capabilities that are often seen as "nice to have" rather than fundamental for success.

That's the advice of John Hillen and Mark Nevins, coauthors *of What Happens Now? Reinvent Yourself as a Leader Before Your Business Outruns You.*

Whether you're an up-and-coming manager or a C-suite executive, it's critical that you know how to reinvent yourself to power through leadership stalls. Hillen and Nevins offer a smart compass to help with the journey.

Rodger Dean Duncan: *In our fast-paced business world, most leaders must deal with challenges of complexity—technology issues, systems and processes, team performance, market forces, etc. But you say the challenges that produce the most career stalls involve sophistication, not complexity. What do you mean by that, and what's an example that illustrates your point?*

John Hillen: Business challenges that add more complexity usually result from simply *more*. More customers, more systems, more products, more supply chain, more employees, more locations, and so on. These challenges can often be met by traditional management changes: new systems, more data or data analytics, different types of reports, a re-organization, or efficiency programs like six sigma or lean manufacturing.

Challenges of sophistication, on the other hand, are different in *kind*, not just scale. These challenges require leaders to reinvent themselves: their skills, mindsets, behaviors, and where they focus time and energy.

Think of the excellent private company CFO who can handle growth in almost all the finance functions: treasury, accounting, vendor management, payroll, invoicing, etc. But when that company raises outside capital and now 80% of the CFO's job is to communicate with and influence investors or regulators, he or she may not be equipped with the very different skills and behaviors needed to address this sophistication challenge.

Duncan: *You say most leaders will inevitably experience a career stall or two and that to deal with such stalls they face a build-buy-bail decision. Please explain.*

Mark Nevins: Paradoxically, stalls are consequences of success: you've done so well that your organization or business has grown and fundamentally changed … but you haven't grown with it. Many stalled leaders go back to the well and tap what's always served them before—their drive, their intellect or knowledge, classic management tools. But often those won't work, because the business is now demanding that they pull back, escalate, and tap into different skills, a new mindset, and a radically changed pattern of behaviors than what made them successful in the past.

In this situation, leaders face the choice to *build* the new skills in themselves; *buy* those skills by hiring (and then staying in their old role, such as the tech company founder who is CTO not CEO); or *bail*, simply taking themselves out of the game.

We believe that if you are thinking about buying or bailing, you may have misunderstood the challenge posed by your stall—or you are backing away from it. Put another way, you may be suffering from a perennial leadership flaw: not realizing that you need to become more sophisticated.

Duncan: *One of the stalls you describe is the result of a dull or disconnected organizational "story." What's involved in getting your story mojo back—fashioning a narrative of purpose and meaning that inspires and engages?*

Hillen: When organizations grow or change, by definition they are doing something new and most often in a changed setting. The old story—one that delivered meaning and purpose across the length and breadth of the organization—may no longer have the same power, especially when the key stakeholder constituencies have gotten larger, more demanding, and driven by varying agendas.

In these situations, the leader must be able to explain, with conviction, the organization's *raison d'etre* now that things have changed. Its vision for the part of the world that it touches; the accomplishments that will fulfill its purpose and make a difference; and the values and behaviors it treasures and promotes.

We demonstrate how to escape what we call the *purpose stall* by showing how to create a meaningful story about the organization's mission, vision, purpose, strategy, and values. We show how you can and must craft a story that carries your people forward on an inspirational, shared, purpose-based quest—a story that can guide people's actions when you are not there to give direction at each new turn.

Duncan: *Some leaders stall because they get out of alignment with their team. What are some early warning signs of a team stall?*

Nevins: Few teams are truly high performing—so if you're struggling with this stall you're not alone. One troubling sign is when team members are not in alignment on enterprise priorities. Most members of senior teams will insist they are, but when we test we find that they don't share the same priorities, or that their individual priorities are taking precedence over company priorities. For example, when you ask them to list what they believe to be the priorities for the team writ large, you get wildly varying answers.

Other warning signs are when members of an executive team resist team reward plans or shared accountability, which betrays a lack of trust and commitment to the team effort. Teams are sure to be in trouble if they cannot seem to collaborate without you, the boss, as an intermediary. You're the referee for everything. Or if they are uncomfortable having honest or difficult conversations with each other (or you) and engage instead in side-channel communications. Another warning sign is when you find yourself unwilling or unable to delegate to your team.

Duncan: *What role can and should a team charter play in the operation of a team?*

Hillen: A team charter is a simple document that helps ensure clarity, buy-in, and commitment from each member of the team on critical matters such as the team's purpose, goals, values, behaviors, and processes. Created by the team itself, the charter binds team members to an agreed-upon framework for how the team will work, prioritize, communicate, make decisions, resolve disagreements, and evaluate team performance. It clarifies areas in which team members need to be mutually accountable versus areas in which they need to individually achieve in their own organizations. A team charter lays out roles, responsibilities, and expectations. It is a social compact between team members as well as an operating guide for how they will interact.

Duncan: *Leaders often struggle during periods of change. And of course, as the saying goes, change is a constant. What are some helpful approaches to engaging people during a major change or implementation effort?*

Nevins: Leading change is perhaps the fundamental role of any leader, and one of the most challenging when faced with mounting sophistication. No matter how many copies of *Who Moved My Cheese* you hand out, people will by nature resist change if they don't understand it, don't trust it, or don't know what it means for them. Ironically your highest performers may be most resistant even unintentionally: they will stall because, in times of pressure, they'll simply try to do what's always worked in the past.

Great change models such as John Kotter's are necessary but not sufficient. In times of change, leaders must foster dialogue. They must listen carefully and patiently. And they must explain the change by appealing to the values of their followers or customers, not just to the bloodless logic of the strategic plan.

Leading change effectively must happen on followers' terms and by assuaging their anxieties about the new future. Every change leader needs to be a CEO—a Chief Explaining Officer.

Personal application:

- If you haven't already experienced a "stall" in your career, what (realistically) could be a stall in your future?

- In dealing with (the probability of) a career stall, what do you see as advantage of a "build" mindset over a "bail" mindset?

- What kind of things can/should you be doing to place yourself in the best position to deal with a career stall?

35

Why Managing Up Is a Skillset You Need

Expert: Mary Abbajay, career coach and author of *Managing Up: How to Move Up, Win at Work, and Succeed with Any Type of Boss*

What you'll learn: If you have a troublesome boss, you need not feel helpless. There are ways to make the situation better.

You've heard it said and you know it's true: People don't quit jobs, they quit bosses.

For many people, the primary ingredient in job satisfaction is not the quality of food in the lunchroom. It's not the office layout or equipment. It's not even the workload, salary, or benefits. It's the relationship with the boss. In fact, one study showed that 65% of workers surveyed would choose a new boss over a pay raise.

Working for a troublesome boss can be nothing short of miserable. A less-than-competent manager can depress your morale, deflate your productivity, and flatten your motivation.

Many organizations still promote people because of their technical success rather than for management skills. To compound the problem, many new managers receive little or no training before jumping into their new roles. This makes for unhappy campers in the workplace.

But you don't have to feel helpless. And looking for another job doesn't have to be your go-to option.

You can improve your situation by working better with the boss you already have.

That's the premise of Mary Abbajay's book *Managing Up: How to Move Up, Win at Work, and Succeed with Any Type of Boss.*

A seasoned leadership development consultant, Mary offers tips on how to deal with some of the most perplexing challenges in the workplace.

Rodger Dean Duncan: *There seem to be countless books, TED talks, workshops and YouTube videos on how to lead and manage downward. But your book provides one of the few treatments on how to manage upward. Why is there such an imbalance?*

Mary Abbajay: The simple truth is that in America, nobody wants to think of himself as a "follower." We are obsessed with leadership. It's part of our cultural and sociological narrative and identity. We talk incessantly about leadership. We teach it, we preach it, we spend more than $14 billion a year on it. But we rarely spend much time discussing or validating the other (and equally important) side of the relationship: followership.

Many of us resist being a follower because we think being a follower is being a patsy. We confuse followership with powerlessness. We conflate it with passivity and submissiveness. We think followership robs us of agency. Nothing could be further from the truth. If we reframe followership from a power construct into a relational construct, we open up a wide world of choice and agency. In a relationship, everybody has agency. So, while we might dislike the idea of being a follower, the truth is that the majority of us spend more of our working time following than leading. Even a CEO must be a follower, too. Everybody has a boss.

Duncan: *Most every leader was once a follower. What are the two or three key things a follower should learn (and practice) in preparation for being an effective leader?*

Abbajay: Leadership in the 21st century is much more about influence than authority, so learning to appreciate and adapt to people with different perspectives, priorities, and personalities is a key skill to develop. Managing up allows you to practice navigating and influencing people who approach work differently than you. Learn how to look beyond your own needs and perspectives and consider the needs and perspectives of others. If nothing else, by managing up, you will learn what kind of manager you want to be and what kind of manager you don't want to be.

Duncan: *For some people, the notion of "managing up" sounds like manipulation or becoming a sycophant. You use the term to mean taking charge of one's workplace experience. When you teach people that this kind of empowerment is a choice, what kind of push-back do you receive?*

Abbajay: People push back for a myriad of reasons. Most of these reasons come down to three things: ego, fixed perspective, and resistance to change.

Ego shows when we get caught up in the need to be right—e.g. we say things like "my boss should...", "my boss needs to...", etc. Our ego prevents us from widening our perspective. We get trapped in our own view, needs, wants.

Our fixed perspective prevents us from considering alternative choices and we may find ourselves trapped in our own cloud of bitterness. While we actually may be totally right, the truth is that your boss isn't going to change. All we can do is change our reaction and our interaction.

Which brings us to the last reason, resistance to change. Managing up requires us to adapt and change our approach. It requires extra effort and moving out of our comfort zone. Change is hard. Most of us would prefer the other to change!

Duncan: *When organizations promote people for technical skills instead of managerial skills, the unintended result can be a technical expert who's a total bust as a manager. What are some proven strategies to "manage up" an incompetent?*

Abbajay: Whether it's due to poor people skills, inexperience, or a lack of managerial aptitude, an incompetent manager doesn't have to derail your career. While specific strategies depend on the individual situation, consider the following approaches:

- **De-escalate your anger:** Having an incompetent boss can be infuriating. But when we operate from a place of anger and resentment, our reptile brain takes over and clouds us from making smart and strategic choices. Let go of the anger and replace it with empathy, compassion, or even humor. Put yourself in your boss's shoes. How would you feel if you were elevated into a position that you weren't qualified for? How would you want your team to treat you? This perspective will enable you to make strategic choices.

- **Diagnose the incompetence:** Try to figure out exactly how the incompetence shows up. Does she lack experience? Does he have poor emotional intelligence? Is her decision-making poor? Does he not hold people accountable? Is she really incompetent or does she just do things differently than you? If you can pinpoint and *prioritize* the problems, you and your team can create targeted strategies to address the deficiency.

- **Compensate and cover**: Once you've pinpointed the major deficiencies, make and enact strategies to compensate. Yes, this requires extra effort. No, this isn't fair. But letting an incompetent boss derail your career isn't fair either. Look for opportunities to shine by doing great work and becoming your boss's biggest asset. Find opportunities to compensate for your boss's weakness. Offer to cover for her when she is out. Proactively provide information that will help him. Offer to take on more responsibility and projects. Use your interactions to help teach them what they need to know.

- **Take the long view:** Try not to worry if your boss gets the credit for your successful projects. Success gets noticed, and in organizations that usually means the team and/or department gets noticed too. Make your boss and your team look good and you will look good as well. Plus, people aren't stupid—everyone probably already knows that you are the success engine behind your incompetent boss.

- **Learn what you can:** If your boss is technically competent, take the time to learn about her technical expertise. Use this opportunity to hone your technical skills.

Duncan: *You've identified ten types of difficult bosses—ranging from the Energizer (lots of enthusiasm but weak follow through) and the Evaluator (driven to producing high-quality work but painfully slow and methodical) to the Narcissist (superficially charming but self-absorbed, power-hungry, and attention-grabbing) and the Impulsive (a whirlwind of ideas but unable to stick to a plan). Yet you say the Micromanager is the most common problem boss. Why is that, and what are some good strategies for dealing with a Micromanager?*

Abbajay: Micromanaging is a common dilemma because it pits two basic human neuropsychological needs against each other: autonomy and control. When our need for autonomy clashes with our manager's need for control we bristle and label it as micromanaging. Navigating this tension is about building trust. In order to gain trust from a micromanager, we have to provide them with what they crave: information, inclusion, and control. Strategies to consider:

- **Anticipate their needs:** The more you can learn about and anticipate your boss's wants, needs, and expectations and proactively address them, the sooner you can remove the need for them to micromanage.

- **Keep them (overly) informed:** Provide regular updates, and status and progress reports before your boss asks for them. This could look like a daily email that lists all your projects and their status, or regularly cc-ing them on emails. Keep them in the loop.

- **Adopt their standards:** Micromanagers often want things done a certain way. If this is the case, then align your work to their preferences. Learn what markers of quality your boss wants/needs and deliver on them. Find out what "right the first time" actually means. If your boss hates the oxford comma, then for goodness sake, drop the oxford comma. Building trust with them means to instill a sense of confidence that you can and will deliver high quality products--aligned with their standards--each and every time.

- **Assess yourself:** If you are the only person being micromanaged, then take a good hard, honest look at your performance. What are you doing or not doing that is preventing your boss (not any boss--this particular boss) from trusting you?

Duncan: *In this #MeToo era, what's your counsel for women trying to "manage up" a male boss?*

Abbajay: Assuming that your male boss isn't sexually inappropriate or predatory, then his gender or "maleness" just becomes another piece of his personality puzzle. Don't make gender an issue if it isn't. Keep your interactions professional. Ensure your boundaries are clear. Be sure you don't inadvertently wade into the grey areas, yourself.

This can be a confusing time for male bosses who are trying to do the right thing. So if you have a good relationship with your male boss, this can be an opportunity to initiate an open and candid dialogue about the #MeToo movement, its implications for working relationships and teamwork at your organization.

Duncan: *You suggest that most people can learn to work well with the boss they have. But what are the signs that it's simply time to move on?*

Abbajay: Nobody should ever work for a boss that is abusive, tyrannical, unethical, or cruel. Nor should you continue to work for someone who doesn't value you or stay in a situation that compromises your health or career. I'm a big fan of knowing when it's time to "grit" or quit. Signs that it's time to move on include:

- You wake up miserable every day and dread going to work.

- Your physical and emotional well-being are being damaged.

- You feel unsafe (physically or emotionally) at work.

- Your stress level is permeating your entire life.

- You spend more time and energy thinking about office politics or strategizing to survive your boss than you do on your work.

- Your self-esteem and self-confidence have plummeted.

- You've tried to make it work, and nothing makes it work.

Remember, when faced with a difficult situation, we have three choices: 1) change it; 2) accept it; or 3) leave it. Sometimes leaving is really the best option!

It's your career and you have the responsibility to make the choice that's best for you.

Personal application:

- Regardless of your own work title, what role does "followership" play in your career success?

- If you feel you have a "problem boss," which of the strategies here are most likely to help you operate productively in your work environment?

- What are the chances that someone needs to "manage up" with you? Which of your behavior might cause that person to feel such a need?

36

How Women Rise: Habits That Curb, Habits That Lift

Experts: Sally Helgesen and Marshall Goldsmith, world-class coaches and co-authors of *How Women Rise: Break the 12 Habits Holding You Back From Your Next Raise, Promotion, or Job*

What you'll learn: Habits that worked early in a career can harm later. Strategic advancement in the workplace requires careful adapting.

Most of the behaviors that hold people back in their careers are gender neutral. Preeminent executive coach Marshall Goldsmith discussed many of them in his international bestseller *What Got You Here Won't Get You There.*

But in today's marketplace, women face some specific—and different—challenges as they try to advance.

Fortunately, Goldsmith has partnered with his longtime colleague Sally Helgesen who's considered the gold standard among women's leadership experts. They've coauthored *How Women Rise: Break the 12 Habits Holding You Back From Your Next Raise, Promotion, or Job.*

This is anything but a woe-is-me-I'm-not-getting-a-fair-shake-because-I'm-a-woman tome. It's a smart and well-researched handbook for women trying to make the next step in their careers—as corporate ladder-climbers or risk-taking entrepreneurs. A key takeaway is that, for women in particular, the very skills and habits that may propel them early in their careers can actually jeopardize their advancement in subsequent stages of their work lives.

Sally and Marshall offer much more than just insights into the *what* of habits that constrain. They provide detailed tutoring on *how* to replace them with behaviors that produce excellent results.

Rodger Dean Duncan: *You've identified 12 habits, or self-limiting behaviors, that you believe hold many women back in their careers and in life in general. How did you develop the list?*

Sally Helgesen: It wasn't scientific, but rather based on our combined 60-plus years of practice, working with women leaders and aspiring leaders all over the world. The 12 behaviors we describe are simply those we find the most likely to get in the way of talented women as they seek to rise. For Marshall, these are behaviors he has worked with as a coach. For me, these are behaviors I've seen in many decades of delivering women's leadership programs and interviewing women leaders.

One thing we want to make clear: these are not uniquely women's behaviors, and we've heard from a number of men who tell us they also identify with some of these behaviors. They are simply *human* behaviors, but they are the ones we see as most likely to get in women's way.

Duncan: *What patterns—and solutions—do you see regarding resistance to change?*

Marshall Goldsmith: Resistance is a powerful force. As humans, most of us are resistant to change because it requires a lot of neural work to practice new behaviors. This consumes energy and takes us out of our comfort zone. But men and women often resist change in slightly different ways.

In my coaching practice, I find that a successful man who resists change often goes through three stages. First, he decides that whoever is suggesting that he change must be confused. Second, he decides that, while the general suggestion for change might be valid, it doesn't necessarily apply to *him* for the simple reason that he's been so successful. Third, he is likely to simply attack the person who suggested that he change, blaming the messenger rather than looking to himself.

Helgesen: A woman who resists change will usually follow a different template. First, she'll react to the suggestion she change by feeling hurt, undervalued, even betrayed. This can be painful and result in a degree of paralysis as she takes the critique to heart. Next, she will ask herself what might have motivated the assessment. What were the circumstances? What perceptions might have been involved? Third, she will begin to examine her own actions and ask how she could have contributed to the assessment.

She may still be deeply resistant to the idea of changing, but she will be open to asking what she might do differently. By internalizing the critique rather than lashing out, she creates a bridge that can enable her to identify constructive action.

Duncan: *How do organizations sometimes make it hard for people to change behaviors?*

Marshall Goldsmith: People get typecast based on the past performance. "Marcy's a good team player." "Samantha's a real workhorse." "Jim's great at building connections, a real schmoozer." Such perceptions are rooted in reality, but they can make it hard for people to change because if they try to branch out their co-workers may push back.

In this way, people can get stuck with an identity that may no longer necessarily serve their interests. For example, for Samantha to move higher, she may need to focus more effort on connecting with people and less on diligently crossing every *t* and dotting every *i*. Yet she may feel reluctant to adopt a new approach for fear she'll disappoint people as she changes.

Duncan: *Self-promotion is uncomfortable for many people. How can a woman call attention to her value and achievements without coming across as bragging at the expense of her team?*

Helgesen: She can present it as information that other people need to know. We have a wonderful story about an engineer named Ellen who learned during a performance review that her boss thought highly of her skills but was concerned that she didn't have enough connections. She felt terrible when she learned this because she'd always thought she was a great connector—a real go-to person who often helped get resources to flow.

For a few weeks she thought about leaving. But she then realized he didn't see her that way because she'd never told him how connected she really was. So she began sending him a two-line email every Friday, simply listing the major people she'd been in touch with during the week. She got no response and was convinced he'd think she was wasting his time or being inappropriately self-promoting. But during her next review he told her that he appreciated what she was doing because it was information she needed to know. So that's one approach.

It's also important for women not to be overly fearful of being perceived as blowing their own horn or being "out for themselves," something most successful men have little problem with. Backing off prematurely is probably worse for a woman's career than stepping a bit over the line.

Duncan: *You tout the value of a good "elevator speech" or statement of purpose. How does this help someone overcome the must-stop habits you write about?*

Goldsmith: Crafting a simple strong elevator speech that describes what you want to achieve in your career is the first step in articulating what you have to offer. The clearer you are about what you have to contribute, the more able you will be to enlist allies who see value in what you are doing and want to help.

Duncan: *Some women are good at building relationships but are less comfortable about leveraging* those relationships. Why is that, and what's your counsel?

Helgesen: One of women's great strengths is their ability to build strong relationships and form deep and lasting bonds. This contributes to their emotional resilience and often makes them connectors within their organizations, go-to people who bring others together. But women don't always benefit from the strong relationships they cultivate and nurture in the workplace because they are reluctant to leverage their relationships, by which we mean engaging others to help them meet either specific or long-term career goals.

When we ask women who are uncomfortable with the notion of leverage, they usually tell us they don't want other people to think they are "using" them. Or they say they want other people to know they value them for themselves, as people, rather than as sources of influence. Or they say they fear being viewed as manipulative or self-serving. As a result, they sometimes fail to reap the benefits of their connections because they are uncomfortable with the transactional nature of quid pro quo that's a standard way of operating in many organizations.

Women we speak with who get caught in this trap often fail to consider that engaging others to help them achieve their own aims can also serve the long-term interests of the other person.

Duncan: *How are allies part of a person's personal brand, and what's the best way to enlist others who can really help you in your career?*

Goldsmith: Your allies or network are your key source of visibility in your organization, community and sector. You are known by the company you keep. This is why over-focusing on developing expertise or doing a perfect job can actually keep you stuck—you may not have the bandwidth for building a strong ally network.

We particularly like to talk about allies because in some quarters there has been an over-emphasis on sponsors and mentors as the only path to success for women. Yes, having a great mentor and sponsor is a huge advantage, but they are not always easy to find. And if the chemistry isn't great, they may not be all that helpful.

So focusing on building allies, informal connections at every level who you keep informed about your work and can rely on for help even as you are a resource for them is a great approach for virtually any woman. It also makes you more likely to attract sponsorship because it makes you more visible and valuable.

Our friend Tom Peters has known a lot of successful people in his very long and distinguished career, and he recently said that what sets them apart is that they spend about 80% of their time building allies. That's a big deal. So it's important to build your ally network from day one.

Duncan: *When you list "Putting Your Job Before Your Career" as a bad habit, you write about the "loyalty trap." What does that mean?*

Helgesen: Research shows that women tend to be extremely loyal to their organizations. This is a good quality, rooted in a strength. But it can hold women back if they feel so loyal to their boss or their team that they decline to pursue opportunities to move ahead. We know an extremely talented associate producer who remained in the job for 11 years rather than the usual five because she felt so much loyalty to her boss. She believed that if she asked him to make connections for her with people who could hire her as a producer, he would think she was being disloyal. What she failed to consider was that *he* had become a producer very early in his career and so would completely understand her wanting to move on. When she finally approached him, he was extremely helpful, though he would not have volunteered because she had become so valuable to his team.

Duncan: *Why does striving for perfection hold people back in their careers?*

Goldsmith: Perfectionism can serve you well early in your career because it supports your doing outstanding work. But it can hold you back as you seek to rise because you are so invested in being precise and correct that you fail to take the kind of risks that characterize strong leaders.

Perfectionism betrays a lack of confidence in your own worth and ability and can make it difficult for you to trust others because you fear they may make mistakes. Perfectionism also creates stress for you as well as those around you. After all, in our many decades of work, we have never met a person who said, "I work with a perfectionistic boss and I love it!"

Duncan: *You write that a good way to overcome self-limiting behaviors is to "unpack" habit clusters. What's a good example of that?*

Helgesen: Many of the behaviors we write about support one another.

For example, Expecting Others to Spontaneously Notice and Value Your Contributions often pairs with Over-focusing on Expertise and Failing to Enlist Allies from Day One.

Perfectionism often results in Rumination. Minimizing often pairs with Putting Your Job Before Your Career.

So we find it very helpful for people to think about how specific habit clusters may impact them so they can figure out the best actions they can take to move forward. What we don't suggest is spending a lot of time trying to figure out why you are prone to certain habit clusters. Instead, taking action to address one behavior or even one part of a behavior at a time enables you to move forward. And enlisting allies to help is even more essential.

Personal application:

- How do you personally respond to change? What effect might your response have on how you are perceived? On your future opportunities?

- What are some ways you can "self promote" without feeling (or coming across as) egotistical or blind to other people's contributions?

- What are you doing to build a network of allies?

Personal Balance

"Balance is not better time management, but better boundary management. Balance means making choices and enjoying those choices."

37

Beat the Time Crunch: Get Better Results at Work, at Home, at Play

Expert: Brian Tracy, personal effectiveness coach, author of *Master Your Time, Master Your Life* and more than 70 other books

What you'll learn: There are no magic formulas for effective time management. But it does require a honest look at our habits and a willingness to make strategic adjustments.

Let's face it. No matter who we are or what our station in life may be, none of us has more than 24 hours a day, 168 hours per week. For most of us, it doesn't seem to be enough.

So the challenge is this: How can we make the best use of that precious and finite resource called time?

It's a question faced by every generation. And in today's world—with its plethora of media and other time-sucking distractions—finding solutions to the time crunch seems more urgent than ever.

It's possible, if not probable, that the simplest solutions make the most sense. That's why I like Brian Tracy's book *Master Your Time, Master Your Life.*

"How did it get so late so soon?" Dr. Seuss asked. It's a question most of us pose every day.

It doesn't have to be that way. Brian Tracy offers workable approaches to investing in simple time management behaviors that pay rich dividends.

Rodger Dean Duncan: *You suggest that most people live in a reactive-responsive mode. How does effective time management help produce better choices and decisions?*

Brian Tracy: Most people live in a "reactive-responsive mode in that they are thrown off by almost every stimulus in their environment, plus whatever pops into their mind at the moment, whether they are working, checking their email or conversing with someone. This is inevitable, unavoidable, and getting continuously worse in our fast-moving world.

Effective time management enables you to impose a sense of control over yourself and your work. By writing down, planning and setting priorities for your day, you can discipline yourself to put a moment of thought between the distraction and the natural impulse to react. You enable yourself to call a brief moment, a "time out," during which you can think with greater clarity about what is more important and what is less important.

Duncan: *What role do clear, written goals play in effective life management?*

Tracy: Clear written goals and plans are more responsible for long-term success than perhaps any other factor. When you're clear about what you really want to achieve in the long term, it's much easier for you to decide what you should do in the short term. Dr. Edward Banfield of Harvard called this "long-term thinking." He said it was more responsible for upward socio-economic mobility than any other factor.

Here's a simple way to change your life: Make a list of ten goals you would like to achieve in the next 12 months, exactly as if you had no limitations. Then ask yourself, "Which one goal on this list, if I achieved it, would have the greatest positive impact on my life?"

Whatever your answer, let this goal become the driving force of your life. Make a list of everything you could do to achieve this goal. Then, resolve to do something that moves you toward this goal every day, seven days a week. This simple exercise has probably been more responsible for great success than any other factor.

Duncan: *You write that today there's a pandemic of poor performance sweeping across the Western world. What do you see as the signs and implications of such a phenomenon?*

Tracy: The pandemic of poor performance that is leading to under-achievement, frustrated expectations for upper mobility, and lower pay is what I call the "attraction of distraction." It's the almost irresistible tendency to react to "shiny objects," especially the ring, bing, or musical sound of email, text messages and phone calls. Each stimulus triggers a shot of dopamine in the brain's pleasure center, almost like the ringing bells and crashing coins of a slot machine paying off, triggering the response, "I wonder what I just won?"

Soon, the impulse to react-respond to stimuli becomes stronger and stronger, and the willpower to resist becomes weaker and weaker. Then the person becomes addicted to the dopamine rush of momentary distractions, all day long, getting less and less done in more and more time.

Duncan: *Many people understand the value of "to do" lists. But you add a fresh wrinkle with what you call the Law of Three. What is that and how does it enhance a person's productivity?*

Tracy: The "Law of Three" is a principle I discovered in working with thousands of business people, entrepreneurs and sales professionals over the years. The way it works is this: If you make a list of everything you do in a week or a month, it will usually contain 20-30 tasks or activities, sometimes more.

But when you analyze your list, you will find that only three of those tasks are responsible for 90% of the value of your contribution to your company, your work, and your personal income.

How do you determine what those three tasks are? Simple. You ask the three "magic questions: Question #1 is: "If I could do only one thing, all day long, which one task would make the greatest contribution to my company?"

Circle that task on your list. It's usually quite clear. (By the way, if you don't know the answer to this question, you had better find out, and fast. You are in great danger of wasting your time, all day long).

Then ask the question two more times: "If you could do only two things, or three things, all day long, which would make the most valuable contribution?"

From this day forward, focus on those three tasks all day long, and dedicate yourself to continuous improvement in each one. This can change your life and make you one of the most valuable people in your organization.

Duncan: *Gary Becker, the Nobel Prize-winning economist, says we don't have an "income gap in our society. We have a "skills gap." What role should continuous learning play in an individual's personal time management?*

Tracy: Warren Buffet, Charlie Munger, and Bill Gates are all lifelong learners. They attribute much of their success to "CANEI," which stands for "continuous and never ending improvement." The reason is simple. In the final analysis, you get paid only for results. If you want to earn more, you must learn more. You must achieve more, better, faster results. You must become more competent at getting the results that people want, need and will pay you for.

The wonderful discovery is that each person has extraordinary abilities, great powers for success and accomplishment that, if they were to tap into and unleash them, would enable them to create the life of their dreams.

Personal application:

- Under what circumstances might you be susceptible to the "attraction of distraction" syndrome? What habits could you adjust (for example, use of social media) to make better use of your time?

- How can you use "the Law of Three" in developing your weekly and daily to-do lists?

- What can you do to ensure that you are engaged in the kind of continuous learning that will pay dividends in your future?

38

Choices to Help You Beat the Genetic Lottery

Expert: Tom Rath, lifestyle researcher and bestselling author of *Strengths Based Leadership* and *Eat Move Sleep: How Small Choices Leader to Big Changes*

What you'll learn: In our information-rich society, many people still harbor dangerous myths about health issues. Gaining reliable data is not only interesting, it can be life-saving.

From millennials to seniors, health has become a near obsession. Health-related discussions are everywhere, from bestseller lists to nightly news stories to political debates to what seems to be every other product commercial on television. As the saying goes, if you don't take care of your body, where else are you going to live?

Tom Rath shares the concern. Considered one of the most influential authors of the last decade, he writes about and studies the role of human behavior in health, business, and economics. He's senior scientist and advisor in the Gallup organization, where he focuses on employee engagement, strengths, and well-being. He's written several bestsellers, including *How Full Is Your Bucket?* and *Strengths Based Leadership*.

I've been particularly interested in Tom's book *Eat Move Sleep: How Small Choices Lead to Big Changes*. So I explored his thinking on a range of issues that affect our health and wellness.

Rodger Dean Duncan: *In your research, what have you discovered to be the two or three most dangerous myths about health?*

Tom Rath: The first myth is that changing your lifestyle requires a major leap such as an entirely new diet. It seems to me that "going on a diet" is almost an admission from the outset that you will stop at some point and revert to less healthful habits. In contrast, what I found is that building small changes into a sustainable lifestyle is what creates meaningful change for good.

Another big myth is that lack of exercise is the primary problem. Personally, I think lack of activity throughout the day is a much bigger issue than people not going to the gym regularly or not exercising for 30 minutes a day. Even if you do have a regular exercise regimen, that will not offset eight or 10 hours of sitting throughout the day.

Then the third myth, that I have been guilty of telling myself for decades, is that I can always "get by" with fewer hours of sleep if I have a lot to get done. The more I studied this research, the clearer it is to me that I actually need more sleep in order to be as effective as possible on important days. Sleep is essentially a positive investment, yet many of us treat it as the first expense we cast aside.

Duncan: *In a nutshell, how are good eating, exercise, and sleeping habits interdependent?*

Rath: It's simply easier to work on all three elements at the same time. If you try to improve in just one of these areas in isolation, you are less likely to succeed compared to what occurs if you work on three of them at once. While the research on this topic is fairly recent, it makes sense when you think about the way a poor night's sleep can lead to bad dietary choices the next morning, less energy for exercise, and so on.

Duncan: *It makes sense that people with overall good health tend to perform better. Specifically, how can good eating, exercise, and sleeping habits help a person who's in a leadership role?*

Rath: The more time I spend on this topic, I think modeling good health will turn out to be one of the most important leadership priorities over the next quarter century. We have developed a lifestyle, at least here in the United States, that is not sustainable for the future. In order to lead us out of this, we need the people who guide the largest social networks in our society to show us how we can fix this colossal problem.

My hope is that some of the best leaders in our society see that they need to be role models and show followers how important it is to eat, move, and sleep well. If leaders prioritize the health and well-being of their people, instead of simply viewing workers as a means to an end, that will be a much greater contribution to society over time.

Duncan: *How can the discipline of maintaining good health habits affect our ability to make good choices in other areas of our lives?*

Rath: Creating good health starts with small choices that make it even easier to create positive change over time. I think the same approach applies to almost any area of life. Our lives are essentially the product of these little moments that accumulate over time. If you are able to improve your health one decision at a time, it should also make it easier to make better choices about what you are doing at work, how you are spending your money, your relationships, and what you do for your community.

Duncan: *Why do so many people talk a good game about health habits while still failing to take very good care of themselves?*

Rath: That may be the biggest challenge we face today, at least in terms of helping people to improve their own health. So many of us are wired to put other people and other priorities ahead of our own basic health. Just think about professionals like nurses and teachers who, almost by nature, put the priorities of patients and students ahead of their own. While this is admirable and done with the best of intentions, there are consequences.

If you fail to take care of your own health first, there is no way you can be as effective for others as the world needs you to be. Whether you are in nursing, teaching, manufacturing, or management, you will have far less energy tomorrow if you do not eat, move, and sleep well today. The people you serve need you to be at your best, and that starts by putting your own health first.

Personal application:

- What modest adjustment(s) could you make in your eating, exercise, and sleeping habits that could improve your health?

- What impact could a measurable improvement in your own health habits have on the people you love the most?

- What can you do on your work team and/or in your larger organization to encourage people to adopt better life balance habits?

39

No Time for Balance? The Solution May Be Simpler Than You Think

Expert: Laura Vanderkam, time management coach, author of *Off the Clock: Feel Less Busy While Getting More Done*

What you'll learn: If you're willing to let go of some popular time management myths, you can discover that getting "off the clock" actually helps you get more done.

Most people who feel the crush of busyness have heard the clichéd advice about time management: "Either run the day or the day runs you." And my favorite, "The bad news is that time flies. The good news is that you're the pilot."

The interesting thing about clichéd advice is that sometimes it's spot-on correct.

Early in my career, my wife and I had two small children. My job and daily commute were stressful. After fighting rush hour traffic, I arrived home one evening and was briefly irritable with our children. I immediately apologized, but still felt bad about my temporary lapse. My wife later asked me "what's going on?" I gave her my usual litany about having so much to do and so little time to do it.

Then my dear wife, a great coach, gave me a gentle lesson that's helped me throughout the four and a half decades since.

"Honey," she began, "I think we live in an age of miracles." I didn't dispute that idea, but asked her to give me an example. "Well," she continued, "I notice that you frequently complain about not having enough time. But I also notice that in the autumn of the year, on Mondays, at precisely 9:00 PM Eastern time, a miracle happens right here in our living room. You somehow *find* three hours to watch Monday Night Football. For a guy who never has enough time, that's truly a miracle."

Then she tied a nice bow on it: "Time really is about making deliberate choices. Like everyone else on the planet, you have only 168 hours a week. Maybe you could re-evaluate the choices you make in how you invest those hours."

Ouch! But don't you love it when someone you trust calls your attention to a blinding flash of the obvious?

Laura Vanderkam expands on this theme in her bestselling book *Off the Clock: Feel Less Busy While Getting More Done.* Her TED talk, "How to Gain Control of Your Free Time" has been viewed more than six million times.

Laura destroys the myth that there's just not enough time in the week for professionals to live happy, balanced, and productive lives. I visited with her to explore her thinking on this ever-popular topic.

Rodger Dean Duncan: *Consistently effective time management is an elusive aspiration for many people. You began your journey by keeping a detailed log of your activities. What did you learn from this practice? Any surprises?*

Laura Vanderkam: If you want to spend your time better, you need to figure out where the time is going now. Otherwise, how do you know if you're changing the right thing? Most people can get a good impression of their lives by tracking a week, but about three years ago, I decided to track my time continuously, keeping a detailed log of all my activities.

This has been a good practice for many reasons. I saw that I did have time to read. I wasn't working as much as I thought. I occasionally have bad nights, but overall I do get enough sleep.

Most importantly, tracking time has helped expand my memory. Now I have a record of exactly how I've spent my time, and I can call these memories back up more easily. Having more memories makes time feel more vast. I see how much choice I have, and making choices skillfully — that is, with a good sense of the data — creates a feeling of time freedom.

Duncan: *It's been claimed that nobody ever said on their deathbed that they wish they had spent more time at the office. How can chronic worka-holics invest more in "off the clock" activities without going on a guilt trip?*

Vanderkam: First, I doubt it's true that no one wished he or she spent more time at the office! Work can be an incredibly meaningful part of life. Also, people sometimes wind up out of the workforce for longer than they mean to due to unemployment or an unexpectedly early retirement, and it derails their financial goals for themselves and their families. That can definitely be a deathbed regret.

That said, if someone is working and would like to have more off the clock time, one great first step is to start planning more fun into life. One reason we keep working at nights or on weekends is that our personal lives aren't compelling enough to stop. I don't think working is a worse choice for time than watching TV. But being intentional about your personal time changes the equation. If you have tickets to a 7 p.m. game you really want to see, you'll probably stop working in time to get there. If you have a hike with your family planned for the weekend, you'll probably check your email less (at least while you're hiking).

In many cases, work expands to fill the available space. When you give it less space, you'll see that the important stuff still gets done, and that can help reduce the guilt.

Duncan: *"Let it go" is one of the approaches you advocate for using time effectively. What kind of choices does "letting go" require?*

Vanderkam: We all have the same amount of time, but people interact with it in different ways. I've found that mental rumination can eat up a lot of time, and keeps people from enjoying the free time they have.

Some people agonize over decisions. They are "maximizers," and want to choose the best possible option. "Satisfiers" (as Barry Schwartz, the psychology professor who studied this phenomenon calls them) set their criteria, and go with the first option that clears the bar. This saves an incredible amount of time, and tends to make people happier, because in most cases, there is no best option. The hotel you choose after three hours of researching is not going to be much better (if it's better at all) than the hotel you choose after three minutes.

I also find that perfectionism eats up a lot of time. People set huge goals for themselves, and then get discouraged and give up. Better to let go of these large expectations and instead aim to make small daily progress—so small, you feel no resistance to the idea. If you want to write a novel, don't set out to write 80,000 words. Set out to write 400 words a day, five mornings a week. Four hundred words is nothing—I've written more than that answering these questions—but this habit will give you a draft in less than a year.

Duncan: *You write that "done is better than perfect because there is no perfect without done." What mental shifts can a perfectionist take to benefit from this view?*

Vanderkam: Nothing is ever truly perfect. I read a lot—as you do!—

and one of the upsides of this is that seeing even classic, great literature has its flaws. I find this encouraging. We're all just trying stuff and seeing what works. Someone struggling with perfectionism can also try realizing this: Your work can't help you until it's out of your head. Once it exists, people can give you feedback, which can help you improve your work over time. You'll also see ways to improve your work. And as people interact with your work, they'll become part of your journey, and want to stay involved in your world. I love that my books are out in the world, becoming part of people's conversations even when I am not physically there. They couldn't do that if I were waiting to achieve perfection.

Duncan: *What are the key to making time for friends, and what role do rich personal relationships play in a person's professional life?*

Vanderkam: For *Off the Clock*, I had more than 900 people with full-time jobs track their time for a day. Then I asked them questions about their time so I could compare the schedules of people who felt time was abundant with people who felt starved for time. I found that people's time perception scores rose in direct correlation with how much time they spent interacting with friends and family. Spending time with people we love energizes us, and that makes us feel like time is rich and full, rather than slipping through our fingers.

We see our families because we live with them, but making time for friends is more complicated. The people who do this well build regular friend get-togethers into their lives. For instance, you commit to meeting for dinner the first Thursday of every month. Or you meet two friends to run at 7 a.m. every Saturday morning. That way, no one has to plan each individual gathering, and people know to plan their lives around it. While it sounds paradoxical that making a time commitment could make you feel like you have more time, I promise it is true!

As for professional relationships, people are people. Work feels more satisfying—and hence people are more engaged—when you spend Monday with people you'd be willing to spend Sunday with too. Viewed from that perspective, chatting with colleagues isn't wasting time. It's actually making you more effective.

Duncan: *What's your bottom-line advice to someone who wants "more time" in their days?*

Vanderkam: One of the best ways to create a sense of time abundance is to plan more adventures into your life. When people say "where did the time go?" what they tend to mean is that they don't remember where the time went. Plan memorable things into your life and you will remember them—and that can make time feel more vast.

Personal application:

- When will you begin keeping a detailed log of your hour-by-hour activities? Today? Tomorrow? The longer you postpone it the more evidence you have that you're not really serious about managing your time.

- How can you *plan more fun* into your life? Who would be a good partner (and reinforcement) in that?

- Which of your routine tasks (including work) could benefit from the *"done is better than perfect because there is no perfect without done"* approach?

Stressed? Tired? Burned Out? Take a Pause

Expert: Rachael O'Meara, manager at Google, author of *Pause: Harnessing the Life-Changing Power of Giving Yourself a Break*

What you'll learn: Regardless of how busy—or indispensable—you think you are, taking a genuine pause could be the very best medicine for your hectic life.

Not long ago I shifted gears on my very busy life. I shut down my consulting practice and put a hold on my writing projects. My wife and I closed up the family home, said goodbye to our children and grandchildren, and headed off to another part of the country.

This was not to be a kick-back-and-relax vacation. It was an uninterrupted twelve months of volunteer missionary service for our church. We sorely missed our family and friends. But it was the best year of our lives. Hard work, yes. But it was *different* work. In addition to the satisfaction of laboring for a cause that's important to us, it was a *change*.

It was a *pause*.

In a world where busyness is often valued more than results, many people are reluctant to take a break, even a short one. After all, who wants to come across as a slacker?

But mastering the art of knowing when to stop, even if only briefly, is a critical ingredient of a life well-lived.

That's the premise of Rachael O'Meara's fine book *Pause: Harnessing the Life-Changing Power of Giving Yourself a Break*.

Are you too busy driving to stop and get gas? This woman's advice is for you.

Rodger Dean Duncan: *In today's fast-paced, competition-driven world, why do so many people seem to have an aversion to taking a time out?*

Rachael O'Meara: Welcome to the Pause Paradox: we value productivity and profits as people and companies, yet we need to ensure we're hitting pause to create sustainable, long-term success at home and at work.

Pausing, or intentionally shifting your behavior, appears counter-intuitive. We often resist pausing to avoid falling behind or looking like a slacker. Instead, consider pausing to enhance creativity or needed downtime, even if it's for a few minutes.

Pro-pause research shows that a wandering mind may facilitate creative problem-solving. Harvard researcher and psychologist Shelley Carson warns us, "A distraction may provide the break you need to disengage from a fixation on the ineffective solution."

Duncan: *Some people are beginning to realize how their lives are consumed by technology. You recommend taking an occasional "digital vacation." What's the science behind that recommendation?*

O'Meara: Taking a digital device pause (DDPs) is one way to detach from technology. As anyone who has vowed to put his or her phone away yet refuses to do so, there is an addictive quality about it all. The reason? When we check our devices, the neurotransmitter dopamine gets released which helps control the brain's reward and pleasure centers, according to *Psychology Today.*

Naturally, as we receive pleasure-inducing digital chimes and comments, we feel good as the physiological response to dopamine in our brain's pleasure center "lights up." This is why it's so difficult to unglue your eyeballs without intentional effort.

Shift your habits by creating rules and boundaries around your screens via daily digital vacations, or pauses. Some ways to try this: limit social media exposure to a set block of time, have a device-free day or time, or put your device away at meals or an hour or two before bedtime. Experiment a bit and decide what works for you.

Duncan: *What are the early warning signs that it's time for a pause?*

O'Meara: There are five key signs you may need a pause. How many of these have you experienced recently?

- **You used to love your job and now you loathe it.** Perhaps you used to thrive on the pressure of your role but it no longer seems worth it. Or maybe you're in a slump. Burnout is a signal to take note of what isn't working and shift.

- **Someone informs you things aren't working out.** It may be a hint or a direct hit.

- **You need a technology intervention**. It's easy to get hooked, and as you know, it's a physiological response to dopamine. When it starts to impact your well-being and relationships, it's time to pause and shift your behavior.

- **A major life event or challenge occurs.** Change is inevitable, and can be a natural inflection point to assess and align with what matters to you.

- **A new opportunity arises.** An irresistible job offer or an invite for a passion project or trip comes along. What is your emotional intelligence telling you? Taking a pause may be exactly what's needed to consider or set course on a new path.

Duncan: *Good decision-making is a crucial part of personal performance. How can a pause help a person resist the temptation to overthink things?*

O'Meara: It's tempting to create a detailed to-do list for some much-needed downtime, taking a pause is an ideal time to stop thinking, and allow some wisdom and answers to emerge. Overthinking can kill just about anything. Pausing is the perfect opportunity to step away from your everyday life and your preoccupied self. Before you face your next time crunch or critical decision, give yourself permission to sit with the idea and step away. One study illustrates that by distancing yourself from a challenge and taking on an observer perspective may enhance your reasoning and lead to insights and new solutions.

Duncan: *How can a person cultivate the skills of "pausing" and thereby derive increasingly more benefit from it?*

O'Meara: Pausing is a state of mind. It can prevent continuing going down a path of burnout, reduce stress, and lead to new insights. Pausing doesn't require financial resources, time, or money. Instead, experiment with different types of pauses. One of the easiest ways to do this is through daily pauses. Here are a few ideas to try. Pick one and practice it within the next thirty minutes.

- **Belly breath pause:** Sit or stand with both feet firmly on the ground and close your eyes if you are comfortable doing so. Place one hand on your diaphragm or heart and slowly inhale, hold your breath, and slowly exhale. Count each inhalation until you get to ten breaths.

- **Digital device pause:** Create a rule to limit or not engage with your devices for a limited time, or not using devices to distract from time with family or friends.

- **The outdoor pause:** Go outside for a walk around the block. Invite a friend for this "nature" pause and explain its purpose and discuss what you experienced.

- **Create a daily one-minute "mindful" awareness pause** while you do something else like brushing your teeth, eating, or walking.

If you already have a daily pause practice, journal about your experience. One study shows that writing about an emotional experience for two minutes a day for two consecutive days improves mood and well-being.

Personal application:

- What rules and boundaries can you set (and follow) to help you manage distractions like digital devices? How can you enlist the help and reinforcement of others?

- Which of the early warning signs of needing a pause have you observed in your life? What's your plan for heeding those signs?

- Do you have a tendency to overthink things? Be honest. Overthinking can be a major deterrent to productivity (and good health).

Bonus Materials

Wisdom, Socrates said, begins with wonder.

LeaderSHOP is for people like you. People who constantly wonder how to improve at learning, leading, serving, listening, planning, and practicing all the behaviors that make for better relationships, more productive work, more satisfying careers, and more fulfilling lives.

The capacity to learn is a gift. The ability to learn is a skill. The willingness to learn is a choice.

You've made the choice to read and digest the ideas offered in *LeaderSHOP*, and we're ready to walk with you on your journey. *LeaderSHOP* is not just a single book. It's an on-going series. Stay tuned for more great content from the world's leading thought leaders.

Register on **www.MyLeaderSHOP.com** and we'll give you early alerts when future volumes of the *LeaderSHOP* series are headed your way. We'll also keep adding to the free bonus materials available to you.

Henry Ford said anyone who stops learning is old, whether 20 or 80. And anyone who continues to learn is forever young.

We hope you'll join us in staying forever young.

Referenced Reading

This is DAY ONE: A Practical Guide to Leadership That Matters, by Drew Dudley

The Why of Work: How Great Leaders Build Abundant Organizations that Win, by David Ulrich and Wendy Ulrich

Discover Your True North, by Bill George

Live Large: The Achiever's Guide to What's Next, by Elizabeth B. Crook

7 Principles of Transformational Leadership: Create a Mindset of Passion, Innovation, and Growth, by Hugh Blane

The Positive Organization: Breaking Free from Conventional Cultures, Constraints, and Beliefs, by Robert Quinn

Great on the Job: What to Say, How to Say It, The Secrets of Getting Ahead, by Jodi Glickman

Simple is the New Smart, by Rob Fazio

A Great Place to Work for All, by Michael Bush

Leading So People Will Follow, by Erika Andersen

You Don't Need a Title to Be a Leader, by Mark Sanborn

Excuse Me: The Survival Guide to Modern Business Etiquette, by Rosanne Thomas

The Profit of Kindness: How to Influence Others, Establish Trust, and Build Lasting Business Relationships, by Jill Lublin

Build an A Team: Play to Their Strengths and Lead Them Up the Learning Curve, by Whitney Johnson

The Agenda Mover: When Your Good Idea Is Not Enough, Samuel B. Bacharach

The Speed of Trust: The One Thing That Changes Everything, by Stephen M.R. Covey

Trust and Betrayal in the Workplace, by Michelle Reina and Dennis Reina

Built on Values: Creating an Enviable Culture That Outperforms the Competition, by Ann Rhoades

Alive at Work: The Neuroscience of Helping Your People Love What They Do, by Dan Cable

TouchPoints: Creating Powerful Leadership Connections in the Smallest of Moments, by Doug Conant and Mette Norgaard

Intelligent Disobedience: Doing Right When You're Told to Do Wrong, by Ira Chaleff

The Leadership Challenge: How to Make Extraordinary Things Happen in Organizations, by Jim Kouzes and Barry Posner

The Bullseye Principle, by G. Riley Mills and David Lewis

Five Stars: The Communication Secrets to Get from Good to Great, by Carmine Gallo

Leadership from the Inside Out: Become a Leader for Life, by Kevin Cashman

START: Punch Fear in the Face, Escape Average, Do Work That Matters, by Jon Acuff

What Happens Now? Reinvent Yourself as a Leader Before Your Business Outruns You, by John Hillen and Mark Nevins

Managing up: How to Move Up, Win at Work, and Succeed with Any Type of Boss, by Mary Abbajay

How Women Rise: Break the 12 Habits Holding You Back From Your Next Raise, Promotion, or Job, by Marshall Goldsmith and Sally Helgesen

Master Your Time, Master Your Life, by Brian Tracy

Eat Move Sleep: How Small Choices Lead to Big Changes, by Tom Rath

Off the Clock: Feel Less Busy While Getting More Done, by Laura Vanderkam

Pause: Harnessing the Life-Changing Power of Giving Yourself a Break, by Rachael O'Meara

Acknowledgments

Many people contributed to the production of this book, notably the dozens of thought leaders who generously talked with me about a wide range of personal development issues. My hearty thanks goes to all of them.

Many others were kind in their endorsements, some published here in the book.

Thanks to Nancy Newland, my friend and graphic designer. She has an unusual gift for translating written words into something that appeals to the eye as comfortably as it entreats the inner ear. In addition, Nancy bursts with joy.

Of course I'm grateful to my friend Marshall Goldsmith for his generous foreword to this book. By any measure, Marshall is a giant in the field of coaching and personal development. Associating his name with this volume is a priceless seal of approval.

As always, I acknowledge the tireless encouragement of dear Rean Robbins, my exceptional wife and sweetheart for these past five decades. Because she knows how much I love the people I serve and how devoted I am to the principles I teach, Rean is my constant cheerleader.

Most of all, I thank God for his goodness and tender mercies. And for the privilege of doing work that really matters.

Rodger Dean Duncan